THE BEDFORD SERIES IN HISTORY AND CULTURE

The Emancipation Proclamation

A Brief History with Documents

Related Titles in
THE BEDFORD SERIES IN HISTORY AND CULTURE
Advisory Editors: Lynn Hunt, *University of California, Los Angeles*
David W. Blight, *Yale University*
Bonnie G. Smith, *Rutgers University*
Natalie Zemon Davis, *Princeton University*
Ernest R. May, *Harvard University*

THE BEDFORD SERIES IN HISTORY AND CULTURE

The Emancipation Proclamation

A Brief History with Documents

Michael Vorenberg

Brown University

BEDFORD / ST. MARTIN'S   Boston ◆ New York

For Bedford/St. Martin's

Publisher for History: Mary V. Dougherty
Executive Editor: William J. Lombardo
Director of Development for History: Jane Knetzger
Senior Editor: Heidi L. Hood
Developmental Editor: Karla Paschkis
Editorial Assistant: Jennifer Jovin
Production Supervisor: Sarah Ulicny
Production Associate: Samuel Jones
Executive Marketing Manager: Jenna Bookin Barry
Project Management: Books By Design, Inc.
Index: Books By Design, Inc.
Text Design: Claire Seng-Niemoeller
Cover Design: Richard DiTomassi
Cover Art: Thomas Nast, *The Emancipation of the Negroes, January, 1863 — The Past and the Future*. Originally printed in *Harper's Weekly*, January 24, 1863, page 56. © Baldev/Corbis.
Composition: Achorn International
Printing and Binding: RR Donnelley & Sons Company

President: Joan E. Feinberg
Editorial Director: Denise B. Wydra
Director of Marketing: Karen R. Soeltz
Director of Editing, Design, and Production: Marcia Cohen
Assistant Director of Editing, Design, and Production: Elise S. Kaiser
Manager, Publishing Services: Emily Berleth

Library of Congress Control Number: 2009932164

Manufactured in the United States of America.

4   3   2   1   0   9
f   e   d   c   b   a

For information, write: Bedford/St. Martin's, 75 Arlington Street, Boston, MA 02116 (617-399-4000)

ISBN-10: 0-312-43581-9
ISBN-13: 978-0-312-43581-3

Acknowledgments

Acknowledgments and copyrights appear at the back of the book on page 164, which constitutes an extension of the copyright page.

Distributed outside North America by Palgrave Macmillan.

Foreword

The Bedford Series in History and Culture is designed so that readers can study the past as historians do.

The historian's first task is finding the evidence. Documents, letters, memoirs, interviews, pictures, movies, novels, or poems can provide facts and clues. Then the historian questions and compares the sources. There is more to do than in a courtroom, for hearsay evidence is welcome, and the historian is usually looking for answers beyond act and motive. Different views of an event may be as important as a single verdict. How a story is told may yield as much information as what it says.

Along the way the historian seeks help from other historians and perhaps from specialists in other disciplines. Finally, it is time to write, to decide on an interpretation and how to arrange the evidence for readers.

Each book in this series contains an important historical document or group of documents, each document a witness from the past and open to interpretation in different ways. The documents are combined with some element of historical narrative—an introduction or a biographical essay, for example—that provides students with an analysis of the primary source material and important background information about the world in which it was produced.

Each book in the series focuses on a specific topic within a specific historical period. Each provides a basis for lively thought and discussion about several aspects of the topic and the historian's role. Each is short enough (and inexpensive enough) to be a reasonable one-week assignment in a college course. Whether as classroom or personal reading, each book in the series provides firsthand experience of the challenge—and fun—of discovering, recreating, and interpreting the past.

Lynn Hunt
David W. Blight
Bonnie G. Smith
Natalie Zemon Davis
Ernest R. May

Preface

The American Civil War and the end of American slavery are two crucial events—the defining events, really—of U.S. history. That the Civil War and emancipation took place at the same time is no coincidence. Slavery was central among the causes of the war, and emancipation was central to the experience of the war. Without slavery, the Civil War would not have occurred—at least at the time and in the way it did. And without the Civil War, slavery and liberation would not have taken the same course. The story of emancipation during the Civil War and Reconstruction embodies all that makes U.S. history fascinating: the struggle to seize and define freedom; the contest between and among peoples of different regions, races, and beliefs; the tension between elite policymakers and ordinary Americans determined to change policy; the conflict between morality and expediency. The story of Civil War emancipation also reveals what makes the *writing* of U.S. history so challenging. How can a historian tell such a complex story? How can a historian capture the role of both elites like Abraham Lincoln and ordinary actors like the slaves themselves in a way that gives credit to all without sacrificing a scholar's critical eye? To examine Civil War emancipation is to appreciate both the substance of and conflict over U.S. history.

This volume introduces students to slavery, the Civil War, and Reconstruction through a focus on the Emancipation Proclamation, a document skimpy in length but powerful in purpose. Although the Proclamation stands at the center of the book, the making and meaning of emancipation is its true subject. The book engages students in the topics that are integral to any survey course on U.S. history, on the American Civil War, or on African American history. Unlike other volumes on Civil War emancipation, this edition provides original documents revealing the actions and ideas of both those who experienced slavery and emancipation and those who crafted the policies that broadened and hindered black freedom. Where other books focus either on Abraham Lincoln and politicians or on enslaved African Americans and their abolitionist allies, this volume opens windows on all of these groups, allowing the reader to understand the complex interaction among them and the crucial roles played by all. This book does not pretend to be comprehensive. To keep the volume brief enough for classroom use, I have omitted some voices of those who commented upon or took part in the process of emancipation. The book does not feature Native Americans and foreigners, for example. Yet it offers a broader spectrum of actors and opinions than any other documentary collection on emancipation.

This edition also introduces students to historiography. Because the history of emancipation has been so contested, it provides an ideal opportunity to expose students to how history is an evolving creation. The essays on emancipation that conclude this volume raise classic questions about historiography. How can historians reach different conclusions from the same sources? How do they reflect the politics of their times? How do they shape the way we think about the past?

The book has two main sections. The Introduction in Part One sets the stage by providing students with background information on the origins of the Civil War, the transformation of the conflict from a war to save the Union to a war for emancipation, and the beginning of Reconstruction. Part Two consists of documents that detail the destruction of slavery. The organization of the documents offers a telling of Civil War emancipation that is both chronological and topical. The selections offer rich possibilities for student discussions and essays. Among the primary sources in Part Two are some of Abraham Lincoln's most famous speeches as well as some of his lesser-known private letters. Included as well are letters and addresses by slaves and former slaves, from famous orators like Frederick Douglass to black soldiers in the rank-and-file of the Union army to female volunteers serving new communities of freed people. Amid these voices are those of southern whites wrestling with the question of whether the Confederacy was defined by slavery and whether slaves might help the Confederate cause. Other documents reveal the thoughts of legal theorists as they ponder the "war powers" of the president. Included in this section are three pairs of images, each pair representing two conflicting views of a crucial moment in the making of African American freedom. Historiography comes into play through two final documents: essays by James M. McPherson and Ira Berlin. They both ask, "Who freed the slaves?" but arrive at different answers.

In the appendix, Questions for Consideration spur students forward in their study, as does a Chronology of Emancipation and a Selected Bibliography of historical works on emancipation during the Civil War and Reconstruction.

A NOTE ABOUT THE TEXT

In all of the documents, I have retained the original spelling, capitalization, and punctuation, providing extra information in brackets or footnotes only in those instances in which a meaning might be unclear or ambiguous.

In almost all cases, the texts reprinted here are from the original sources. The exceptions are texts written or spoken by Abraham Lincoln, all of which come from Roy P. Basler, ed., and Marion Dolores Pratt and Lloyd A. Dunlap, asst. eds., *The Collected Works of Abraham Lincoln* (New Brunswick, N.J.: Rutgers University Press, 1953).

ACKNOWLEDGMENTS

I owe thanks to many institutions and individuals. I am grateful to the Brown University Library for helping to locate and in some cases reproduce texts and images appearing in this book. Authors and publishers have been generous in granting the rights to reproduce their work. I have been fortunate in having expert research assistants to help me track down, reproduce, and interpret the documents—Neko Catanzaro, Sara Damiano, Peiling Li, and Emily Shapiro.

I have relied on a number of existing documentary collections to guide me to original sources reprinted here. Of these collections, the most important have been the volumes published by the Freedmen and Southern Society Project at the University of Maryland, especially the books in the series *Freedom: A Documentary History of Emancipation, 1861–1867* (Cambridge: Cambridge University Press, 1982–). Like all historians, I am grateful to the Project's scholars, who have unearthed treasures which have enriched our understanding of slavery and emancipation. My debt to these scholars is particularly great, as their work provided a map to the archives without which I could not have completed this project.

At Bedford/St. Martin's, Heidi Hood, Patricia Rossi, Mary Dougherty, William Lombardo, and Jennifer Jovin kindly took an interest in the project and never lost faith in it. My development editor, Karla Paschkis, saved me from numerous errors, as did the editors who were responsible for copyediting and production—Emily Berleth at Bedford/St. Martin's and Nancy Benjamin and Barbara Jatkola of Books By Design.

I am grateful as well to reviewers of the preliminary manuscript: Angela Boswell, Henderson State University; James O. Horton, George Washington University; Robert E. May, Purdue University; James

Oakes, The Graduate Center, CUNY; and Charles W. Saunders, Kansas State University.

Finally, I owe special thanks to two great historians: David Herbert Donald, who sparked my interest in this book's subject more than twenty years ago; and David W. Blight, who helped keep me engaged in the topic and nurtured the kernel of an idea that has become this book.

Michael Vorenberg

Contents

4.   African Americans and Military Service   **79**

5.   The Confederacy Considers Emancipation   **93**

THE BEDFORD SERIES IN HISTORY AND CULTURE

The Emancipation Proclamation

A Brief History with Documents

PART ONE

Introduction: The Making and Meaning of Emancipation

If there was one defining moment of the American Civil War, it was Abraham Lincoln's signing of the Emancipation Proclamation on January 1, 1863. The moment was not as dramatic as the three-day battle at Gettysburg later that year. Nor was it as poetic as the address that Lincoln delivered at Gettysburg four months after the battle. Historian Richard Hofstadter later mocked the Proclamation's legalistic language, claiming that it gave the document "all the moral grandeur of a bill of lading."[1] Despite its literary weaknesses, the Proclamation, by declaring emancipation a Union war aim, did more than any other act or action during the war to signal a shift in the conflict and in the direction of the United States.

Before emancipation became an explicit Union aim, slavery's death grip on the country remained firm. As late as December 1, 1862, a mere month before he signed the Proclamation, Lincoln had proposed amendments to the U.S. Constitution that might have allowed slavery to exist in the country until 1900 (Document 20). Meanwhile, a constitutional amendment approved by Congress in March 1861 that protected slavery where it existed for eternity remained before the states, awaiting ratification. Lincoln had promoted the measure in his First Inaugural, the state legislatures of Maryland and Ohio had quickly voted for its ratification, and the Illinois state constitutional convention in 1862 had endorsed it. The amendment remained before the states during the Civil War and after: The Constitution gives Congress no authority to recall an amendment. But the measure was rendered meaningless by the Thirteenth Amendment, ratified in December 1865, which prohibited slavery. Well before the ratification of the Thirteenth Amendment, however, the Emancipation Proclamation declared what many had believed since the war began: Slavery was on a path to destruction.

SLAVERY, FREEDOM, AND THE COMING OF THE CIVIL WAR

Prior to the Civil War, American leaders had gone to extraordinary lengths to keep the institution of slavery from dividing the nation. Some of the delegates to the nation's constitutional convention of 1787 had suggested abolishing the institution, but the knowledge that pressing such proposals would dissolve the convention led those inclined against slavery to accept a number of measures that helped preserve the institution well into the nineteenth century. Among these was a clause requiring fugitive slaves to be returned to their owners, a clause that Congress invoked when passing the first Fugitive Slave Act in 1793. The Constitution also prohibited the abolition of the transatlantic slave trade for twenty years after the Constitution's ratification, and it enhanced slaveowners' power in the House of Representatives by counting every slave, whom the law generally treated as a nonperson, as three-fifths of a person for the purposes of congressional representation. Perhaps most significant, at least in hindsight, the Constitution gave no explicit power to Congress over slavery in the states. Most lawmakers in the nineteenth century read that omission as evidence that only state lawmakers, or slaveowners themselves, could free slaves. However, the Constitution did make some concessions to those opposed to slavery. Those wanting a prohibition of slave importation from abroad could look forward to 1808, when Congress would be able to abolish the trade — which it did. Those wanting the Constitution to give the national government some power to destroy slavery were heartened that Congress had sole jurisdiction over the federal territories and the nation's capital, which in 1790 became the District of Columbia, carved from two slave states, Maryland and Virginia. If Congress wished to abolish slavery in these areas, no state law could stand in its way. Finally, those who were embarrassed that slavery would still exist in the country, no matter how much the

Constitution weakened it or set it on the road to destruction, could take solace in the fact that the document never used the word *slave, slaves*, or *slavery*. "Person held to Service or Labor" was as close as the document came to referring to the institution directly.

Although the Constitution invested the national government with new powers, lawmakers generally agreed that the power to regulate and abolish slavery lay with the states, not with the national government. States had made very different choices about how to use that power. When the Revolution began, slavery was legal in all the states, including those in the North. By the turn of the nineteenth century, however, all the northern states had adopted emancipation measures. Abolition was gradual in most of the northern states—the census of 1860 recorded a few slaves in New Jersey, for example—and slaveowners in the North usually received some sort of compensation for the loss of their human chattel. Most often, compensation took the form of forced apprenticeships: Newly freed African Americans would have to serve their former masters for a fixed term of years and for a set number of hours every week. Former masters in the North could no longer buy and sell their former slaves, but they still possessed much of their labor and could discipline them with impunity—though for a finite period only. Meanwhile, in the upper Midwest, an area known as the Northwest Territory until the mid-1800s, slavery was also on the road to destruction. Because of the Northwest Ordinance of 1787, which was originally drafted by Thomas Jefferson and prohibited further importation of slaves into the territory, all the new states in the region adopted antislavery constitutions. In the South, however, antislavery activists failed to make much headway. Abolitionists met defeat in the debates on emancipation that took place in the southern states. Rising profitability of the institution, created by new technology such as the cotton gin and more brutally efficient labor practices, made it increasingly unlikely that southern state lawmakers would voluntarily abolish slavery.

Not only did slavery in the South fail to wither; it became increasingly regimented and inhumane, especially in reaction to abolitionist pressures and slave revolts throughout the Atlantic world. In all of the European countries that possessed colonies in the western Atlantic and Caribbean, antislavery activists battled for abolition both at home and in the colonies. Aside from offering moral and economic reasons for emancipation, abolitionists argued that a race war might result if blacks were kept in bondage. For evidence, they pointed to the 1791 slave uprising in St. Domingue, the French colony on the western side of the island now known as Hispaniola.* Blacks there eventually established the independent republic of Haiti in 1804. As England and France in the early 1800s moved toward abolishing slavery in their colonies (Spain and Portugal would not act until after the Civil War), southern slave-owners increasingly pushed for state legislation insulating the institution from abolition. In Virginia, the site of slave rebellions in 1800 and 1802, state laws in the early decades of the nineteenth century prohibited owners from emancipating their slaves unless they sent the freed people out of state. Later episodes of slave resistance, such as the foiled plot of Denmark Vesey in South Carolina in 1822 and the bloody rebellion led by Nat Turner in Virginia in 1831, led to an even firmer legal clampdown. Laws prohibiting owners from teaching slaves to read or allowing them to carry firearms now cropped up on the statute books alongside older laws denying slaves the right to marry or earn wages. As slavery decayed throughout much of the Western Hemisphere, it became more vibrant than ever in the American South.

Northerners took note of slavery's vitality and repressiveness in the South, but few did anything to strike directly at the institution, for they tended to conflate its continued existence in the South with the stability of the Union. The exception was an ever-expanding group of northern abolitionists, which included men and women of all races: former slaves, transplanted southern whites, white middle-class workingmen and their wives, and a growing number of evangelical Christian men and women, who saw slavery's crushing of each individual human soul as a sin against God. Their main strategy was to use "moral suasion" against slavery—to shame slaveowners and their northern allies into freeing the slaves. They tended to be nonviolent and distrustful of government action. It was the national and state governments, after all, that had allowed slavery to thrive. They would never have imagined that a U.S. president might one day issue an emancipation proclamation or that the nation would ratify a constitutional amendment prohibiting slavery. The printing press, not the law, was their favorite weapon. They printed antislavery petitions and sent them around the country, even into the

---

*St. Domingue appears in some texts as Saint-Domingue or Sainte-Domingue, French names for the colony, or St. Domingo or Santo Domingo, the Spanish versions of the name. All of the names refer to the same place, which in this book is referred to as St. Domingue. St. Domingue was originally a Spanish colony—the western part of the island called La Española by Christopher Columbus in 1492 and later named Hispaniola by the English. By 1700 the French had taken control of the colony. After the revolution there and the establishment of the independent republic of Haiti in 1804, writers continued to use any of the country's former names to refer to the nation or to the entire island where it was located.

heart of the Slave South. They printed antislavery pamphlets and newspapers. Most famous among the abolitionist printers was the Bostonian William Lloyd Garrison, whose newspaper, the *Liberator*, first appeared in 1831 and ran until 1865, when the Thirteenth Amendment outlawed slavery.

At every turn, abolitionists were met by vocal, sometimes violent opposition. In Boston in 1835, anti-abolitionists dragged Garrison through the streets. That same year, a mob led by a former governor of South Carolina broke into the post office in Charleston and burned bags of antislavery petitions. Two years later, anti-abolitionists murdered Elijah Lovejoy in Alton, Illinois, and destroyed his printing presses, which he had used to publish an antislavery newspaper. Politicians who were morally opposed to slavery, such as Abraham Lincoln, were disgusted by the violence, yet they also frowned upon abolitionists who were willing to disrupt the peace in the name of their cause. An astute lawyer who revered the Constitution, Lincoln believed in the rule of law. Southern states had the power to make whatever laws regarding slavery they wished, and abolitionists had no business either breaking the law or encouraging others to do so. By the same logic, abolitionists were out of line when they took aim at northern state laws that discriminated against free African Americans or denied them the vote. These "black laws," especially prevalent in the Midwest, rarely provoked the ire of mainstream politicians such as Lincoln, and most remained on the books until the Civil War era.

Although most antislavery activists at first refrained from formal political action, by the late 1830s the lack of visible results led a faction to create a new, abolitionist political party, the Liberty Party. One politician deeply affected by this new turn was John Quincy Adams, the former president who was now serving as a congressman from Massachusetts. Adams never joined the Liberty Party, although he shared many of its views. In 1836, Adams spearheaded a successful eight-year campaign to overturn the congressional gag rule, which limited congressmen's power to read antislavery petitions on the floor of the House of Representatives. Throughout the late 1830s and early 1840s, Adams frequently suggested that the national government might indeed have the power to emancipate slaves in the southern states if there was a national emergency or the country was in a state of war. This "war power" justification of national emancipation, which Adams had rejected twenty years before when he served as secretary of state, would become the constitutional basis of Lincoln's argument for the Emancipation Proclamation twenty years later.[2] Adams's argument aside, northerners' acceptance of southern states' power over slavery was part of the political culture that held the Union together.

Also holding the Union together was the ambiguity over the future of slavery in the federal territories to the west. Although Congress had prohibited further importation of slaves to the Northwest Territory in the Northwest Ordinance of 1787—before the Constitution had been adopted—it said nothing later about slavery in the other western territories, including the vast 830,000 square miles of the 1803 Louisiana Purchase. Congress admitted a roughly equal number of slave states and free states in the thirty years after the Constitution was ratified, but it did not attempt to dictate the fate of slavery in the West until 1819, when debate began over the admission of Missouri. The legislation that resulted, the Missouri Compromise of 1820, admitted Missouri as a slave state and Maine as a free state, and it prohibited slavery in the existing western territories north of latitude 36°30'. The compromise suggested that those who favored slavery and those who opposed it would control roughly equal amounts of territory, but it left open the possibility of further conflict. What would happen if the population of one side outgrew the population of the other, wrecking the balance in the House of Representatives between antislavery and proslavery congressmen? The balance in the Senate likewise could tip if more states were created in one section than the other. The Missouri Compromise made future conflict inevitable, even as it helped preserve the Union.

The linchpin of the machinery that kept slavery from splitting the Union was the Fugitive Slave Law of 1850. The first such law was adopted in 1793 and gave slaveholders the right to recover slaves who had escaped—even if they had fled to free states. But the law was ambiguous on some points. For example, to what extent were free states' authorities obliged to return fugitive slaves? Slaveowners were furious at the occasional abolitionist rescues of fugitives who had been found and locked up in northern jails, and increasing numbers of northerners were upset by the way the law nationalized slavery by allowing slave catchers to come into free communities. The Fugitive Slave Law of 1850, part of a set of agreements in Congress that would come to be known as the Compromise of 1850, was less ambiguous but even more polarizing. It compelled state authorities to enforce the law and provided judges with financial incentives not to proclaim the freedom of African Americans accused of being fugitives. Northerners disgusted by the law and by the sensational cases it produced—such as that of Anthony Burns, an African American living in Boston for years as a free man, who was captured, tried, and marched through the city streets by federal troops escorting him to a ship bound south back to slavery—swelled the litionists' ranks. It was this new Fugitive Slave Law that spurred Harriet Beecher Stowe to write *Uncle Tom's Cabin*, a bestseller that condemned both northern apathy toward slavery and southern support of it. Yet most white northerners, including Abraham Lincoln, accepted the Fugitive Slave Law as one more necessary compromise for the sake of preserving the Union.

By the time the Fugitive Slave Law had been adopted, however, the bonds of Union had begun to unravel. In 1846, President James K. Polk incited a war with Mexico, a conflict against which Lincoln, a Whig congressman from Illinois, voiced his disapproval. The war raised the prospect that the United States would gain vast new territories in the West. Mexico had abolished slavery in 1829, but would the United States lift the ban? The likelihood that a war with Mexico would lead to a devastating political fight over whether slavery could exist in the land acquired from the conflict led Ralph Waldo Emerson to predict that "Mexico will poison us."[3] To head off such a possibility, Senator David Wilmot, an antislavery Democrat from Pennsylvania, proposed a "proviso" barring slavery from territories acquired from Mexico. Opposition to the measure came mostly from southerners of both main political parties, the Democrats and the Whigs. They saw the Wilmot Proviso as part of a long-term abolitionist plot to use any means necessary to destroy slavery and bring southern whites under northern authority. When Wilmot's measure was defeated, antislavery activists warned of a southern plot to take over the West for slavery. Wilmot and other antislavery Democrats, along with splinter groups from the Liberty and Whig parties, joined together to create the Free Soil Party, which was committed to keeping slavery confined to the South and out of the West. A generation earlier, Thomas Jefferson had warned that if political parties came to represent sections of the country rather than drawing their membership from all regions, the Union would be doomed. The emergence of the robust Free Soil Party, an exclusively northern organization that ran a presidential candidate in 1848, suggested that Jefferson's worst fears had been realized.

In fact, the Union was able to endure long beyond the creation of a northern antislavery party. The Democrats continued to draw strength from all sections of the Union, and the Whigs remained a viable national party until the mid-1850s. Also, by the mid-1850s a new national party had emerged, the American Party, commonly called the "Know Nothings." Anti-Catholic and anti-immigrant in its orientation, the American Party drew most of its strength from northerners concerned about the recent tide of immigrants from Ireland and Germany, who had arrived

...hores. But the party aimed to gain strength in the ...well have come to replace the Whigs as the main ...ompetition with the Democrats had it not been for ...giving politics the sectional basis that Jefferson had

The ... ...ese events was the Kansas-Nebraska Act of 1854, a measure that struc.. a deathblow to any further compromise over slavery in the West. The act repealed the Missouri Compromise and allowed the people of any remaining territory within the former Louisiana Purchase, even one above latitude 36°30', to vote slavery in or out. This was the principle of "popular sovereignty" touted by Stephen A. Douglas, the Democratic senator from Illinois. The violation of the old territorial compromise led antislavery Whigs such as Lincoln to join with Free Soilers and other antislavery politicians in the creation of a new, exclusively northern party: the Republicans. From 1854 to 1856, the Republicans and Know Nothings vied to succeed the defunct Whig Party as the main party to compete with the Democrats. Both the Republicans and the Know Nothings played on northerners' nativism—their fear of immigrants, especially Catholics—and both had constituencies generally opposed to the spread of slavery. But the Republican Party proved to be more effective at convincing northerners that it was the better safeguard against a "Slave Power" of slaveowners and their northern allies bent on seizing national power and subverting American democracy.

For evidence of the Slave Power, Republicans pointed to Kansas. There proslavery "ruffians" poured into the territory to turn it into a new state where slavery would be legal. In 1856, they brazenly sacked the antislavery town of Lawrence. They cheered when they heard the news from Washington, D.C., that Congressman Preston S. Brooks of South Carolina had beaten Senator Charles Sumner of Massachusetts nearly to death on the Senate floor after Sumner had insulted Brooks's relative during a speech called "The Crime against Kansas." As Republicans such as Abraham Lincoln denounced this "crime"—and the attack on Sumner—they rose to prominence. Their opponents spoke of the guns and fighting men that eastern antislavery activists had sent west, arguing that abolitionists were equally responsible for the war now known as "Bleeding Kansas."

Out of the cauldron of Bleeding Kansas emerged John Brown. A deeply religious egalitarian, Brown had long despised slavery but had turned violent against it only when he traveled to Kansas, where he oversaw the massacre of five supposedly proslavery settlers at Pottawatomie Creek and then, along with his sons, declared war on all supporters of slavery in the region. The fight over Kansas had not only created the most successful sectional party in the nation's history, the Republicans, but it had also propelled into the spotlight two of slavery's most famous foes, John Brown and Abraham Lincoln.

Three years after the Kansas-Nebraska Act, in the *Dred Scott* decision of 1857, the U.S. Supreme Court opened the door even more widely for slavery to enter the territories. The Court, headed by Chief Justice Roger B. Taney, a slaveowner from Maryland, declared not only the Missouri Compromise but also popular sovereignty unconstitutional. Congress had no power to prohibit slavery in the territories, Taney ruled. Nor could it approve territorial constitutions that outlawed slavery. The decision also affirmed earlier court rulings allowing slaveowners to take their slaves into free states without restriction or threat of having their human property liberated. That raised the prospect of slaveowners establishing settlements of slaves in free states—in other words, the reintroduction of slavery in the North. Most offensive to African Americans was the part of Taney's opinion declaring that blacks could not be citizens. He based his ruling on his belief that blacks at the time of the Constitution's creation "had no rights which the white man was bound to respect" and were "altogether unfit to associate with the white race."[4] Their status, Taney argued, had not changed since then. Lincoln denounced the decision but refused to take any firmer action against slavery. Instead, he continued to focus on keeping slavery from the West, devoting his energies to the group he believed would best achieve that goal: the Republican Party. Calling the *Dred Scott* decision less than a "settled doctrine," Lincoln looked forward to a time when the Republicans would have enough power to push doctrine in a new direction.[5]

That opportunity came in 1860, when a sectional split in the Democratic Party made Republican victory in the presidential election a genuine possibility. The Republicans nominated Abraham Lincoln, who had earned a reputation as a moderate because of declarations that he would not touch slavery where it already existed and that he would uphold the Fugitive Slave Law. In his campaign, Lincoln continued to deny that he would do anything against slavery beyond restricting it from the territories. He also never missed an opportunity to distance himself and his party from John Brown, who had regained national attention in 1859 with his raid on the federal armory at Harpers Ferry, Virginia, an attack meant to incite a slave uprising. Lincoln denounced Brown as a fanatic and declared that no Republican approved of the violent strategy adopted by Brown, whose favorite biblical passage was "Without shedding of blood there is no remission of sin" (Heb. 9:22). Little could Lincoln have suspected that he would deliver a similar message less than five years later when, in his Second Inaugural (Document 45), he suggested that the blood spilled during the American Civil War was a sort of penance for slavery—a "woe due to those" who had blighted the land with bondage.

MAKING A WAR FOR EMANCIPATION

Southern whites reacted with horror to Lincoln's election. Here was a president-elect who had explicitly said that slavery was an immoral institution, even as he added dubious promises not to touch it where it existed. Worse, he had been elected without victory in even one slave state. Now that he was to be president, he could renounce all his campaign promises regarding slavery and the South. He could use patronage—the power to appoint federal officeholders throughout the country—to build a loyal cadre of powerful officials in every southern state. Enough southerners came to assume the worst of the new president that within three months of his election, the seven states of the Deep South seceded and created the Confederate States of America. (Four other southern states joined later that spring.) The Confederates elected Jefferson Davis of Mississippi as president and Alexander Stephens of Georgia as vice president. A convention of the new nation drafted a constitution that explicitly protected slavery. Before the Confederacy was two months old, Vice President Stephens declared in a widely circulated speech that slavery was the cornerstone of the Confederacy (Document 4).

In his First Inaugural of March 4, 1861 (Document 5), Lincoln restated his commitment to noninterference with slavery where it already existed, as well as his intention to enforce the Fugitive Slave Law. He even went so far as to endorse the constitutional amendment that would protect slavery in perpetuity.

Lincoln may have denied that his election signaled the end of slavery, but many African Americans believed otherwise. Days after the First Inaugural, eight runaway slaves arrived at Fort Pickens, a federal fort in Florida. The commander there informed the U.S. War Department that the slaves were "entertaining the idea that we were placed here to protect them and grant them their freedom."[6] The commander, like Lincoln, believed that federal authorities had a duty to enforce the Fugitive Slave Law. He made sure that the slaves were returned to their owners.

In the first months after his inauguration, Lincoln held to his campaign promise that he would not interfere with slavery where it existed.

In addition to endorsing the proposed constitutional amendment protecting slavery, Lincoln told his subordinates that Union armies must be particularly careful not to threaten slavery in the Border States, whose allegiance the president desperately needed. If the slave states of Delaware, Maryland, Kentucky, and Missouri seceded and joined the Confederacy, restoring the Union might be impossible.

Yet in promising the slave states in the Union that the national government would not interfere with slavery there so long as they remained loyal to the Union, he implied that he would not protect slavery if they seceded. The same held true for the states that already had seceded. Their disloyalty to the Union, in Lincoln's view, weakened if not revoked his obligation to protect slavery in those states.

Lincoln therefore did not object when one of his commanders, General Benjamin F. Butler, refused to return three slaves to their masters when they arrived at Fortress Monroe, the post he commanded in Virginia (Document 7). Butler rightly understood that every slave returned to a Confederate was a potential laborer against the Union. So he refused to return escaped slaves to their owners, instead declaring them "contrabands." The term referred to any enemy property that, when seized, could be used against the enemy. Butler was most likely not the first commander to use the term to describe escaped slaves, but news of his action spread widely and became the best-known example of how Union forces in the field could undermine slavery. Some commanders acted out of moral outrage against slavery; others simply saw a way of weakening the Confederacy. Regardless of their motives, by calling slaves contrabands, a name usually reserved for weapons and supplies, Butler and other military personnel invoked the insidious doctrine that slaves were property, not humans. With the will and calculation of humans, slaves had run from their masters to Union lines, but it was only as property that Union armies granted them asylum.

Congress followed the lead of Union military officials, though slowly. In late July 1861, a few days after the Union defeat at the Battle of Bull Run (later known as the First Battle of Bull Run, or Manassas), Congress passed the Crittenden Resolution declaring that the object of the war was simply the restoration of the Union, not the disruption of states' "established institutions" — meaning slavery. Just two weeks later, however, Congress passed what became known as the First Confiscation Act, which legalized the army's contraband policy by authorizing the seizure of slaves used by Confederates in military operations against the Union. A little less than a year later, in July 1862, Congress took further steps. First, it passed the Militia Act, authorizing the military to employ blacks; African Americans in military service would be emancipated, as would any wives and children owned by anyone in rebellion. In the Second Confiscation Act, Congress declared free all slaves owned by anyone in rebellion. Although these acts represented major blows against slavery, congressmen claimed that they did not violate states' rights. The acts targeted treasonous *people*, not states. Congress did not split legal hairs in this way when it acted in places where, according to Republicans at least, the Constitution gave the federal government exclusive jurisdiction: the District of Columbia and the territories. In April 1862, Congress abolished slavery in the District; two months later, it abolished slavery in the territories.

Lincoln signed all of the congressional legislation against slavery, but he also made sure that the legislation contained provisions for compensation to loyal owners for the loss of their slaves. As a lawyer, Lincoln took seriously the Fifth Amendment's prohibition against taking property without just compensation. He won the battle for compensation in the act emancipating slaves in the District—the law paid loyal owners the supposed market value of their slaves—but he lost it in the confiscation acts, neither of which explicitly provided for compensation.

Lincoln's greatest concern about emancipation remained that it would lead to the secession of the slave states still loyal to the Union. Even as he supported Congress and the military in its moves against slavery in the Deep South, he demanded a softer approach in the Border States. In September 1861, after John C. Frémont, the presidential candidate of the Republican Party in 1856 and now a military commander in the West, declared slaves in the Union state of Missouri emancipated by martial law, Lincoln urged him to modify the order. Frémont refused. Lincoln rescinded the order and then, two months later, removed Frémont from command. From the start of the war, Lincoln urged representatives from the Border States to abolish slavery by state action, suggesting that they could make emancipation gradual if they wished. Congress cooperated by adopting legislation pledging compensation to slaveowners in any Border State that abolished slavery. But in the first two years of the war, none of the Border States budged on emancipation, and by the summer of 1862, Lincoln doubted that his emancipation plan for the Border States would work.

Lincoln believed, correctly, that white racism was one of the causes of the Border States' reluctance to take up his offer of compensation. Having been born in the slave state of Kentucky and come of age in Indiana and Illinois—states with discriminatory "black laws" and a history of violence by whites against blacks—Lincoln assumed that most whites in the Border States, indeed most whites throughout the country, were unwilling to live peaceably with newly emancipated African Americans. In his opinion, blacks deserved equal treatment even if, as he believed, slavery had diminished their intellectual capacity. Believing that African Americans might fare better if they left the country, and hoping that the prospect of black emigration might make emancipation more palatable to whites in the Border States and elsewhere, Lincoln promoted plans to colonize blacks abroad.[7]

The idea of black colonization was as old as the Republic. Supporters of colonization included George Washington, Thomas Jefferson, and James Madison. Some who advocated colonization simply wanted the country rid of darker-skinned people. Others, like Lincoln, saw the cause as a benevolent endeavor to protect blacks from white racism and their inexperience in living in a free society. Most African Americans opposed colonization, arguing that they had as much right as whites to claim the United States as their home. But some supported the idea as the best route to security and community.

Colonization efforts initially focused on Africa. In 1816, the American Colonization Society was founded; its mission was the voluntary resettlement of black Americans in Africa. In 1821, the United States established the colony of Liberia, on the west coast of Africa, as a destination for black emigrants from the United States. In 1847, fearing that it would be annexed by England, Liberia became an independent country. By then, funding for colonization had dried up, and a vibrant abolitionist movement in the North, led by both white and black Americans, had turned against colonization.

Yet a small number of Americans, including Lincoln, continued to support the voluntary emigration of African Americans. When Lincoln became president, he received many proposals for black emigration, most of them aimed not at Africa but at Central or South America. The successful establishment of Haiti, an independent republic founded after the slave uprising in the French colony of St. Domingue, served as a model for potential black republics elsewhere. Or perhaps African Americans might simply emigrate to Haiti. That was one of the reasons the Lincoln administration became the first in American history to recognize Haiti as a nation and receive its ambassador. Lincoln also appointed commissioners to drum up support for emigration among free African Americans, and he urged Congress to appropriate funds for colonization. Congress obliged. In its act of April 1862 emancipating the slaves of Washington, D.C., Congress appropriated $100,000 to fund the emigration of any of the newly freed slaves—about three thousand in all—who wished to settle abroad. Three months later, in the Second

Confiscation Act, Congress appropriated another $500,000 for colonization. Yet funds for colonizing ex-slaves abroad did no more to persuade the Border States to abolish slavery than did promises of compensation to owners.

By the summer of 1862, Lincoln had grown increasingly desperate for the Border States to abolish slavery. He knew that emancipation by state action there would help demoralize the states that had seceded. A great military victory over the Confederacy would also weaken the will of the secessionists, but so far Lincoln's generals had failed to deliver a grand stroke, such as the capture of the Confederate capital at Richmond. The president might have to follow the advice of those who counseled a more aggressive strategy against the Confederacy, one that included a presidential order of emancipation. In May 1862, when the Union general in the Southeast, David Hunter, proclaimed that all the slaves in his district would be freed and enlisted, Lincoln countermanded the order and wrote that he alone, as commander in chief, could "declare the Slaves of any state or states, free."[8] Such a declaration was obviously on his mind, but it might drive the Border States into the Confederacy. In a meeting with Border State congressmen in July 1862, Lincoln urged his compensation plan one more time, warning that if the states did not adopt it, slavery there might soon "be extinguished by mere friction and abrasion—by the mere incidents of war."[9] Lincoln was not merely speculating. Just after the Border State representatives left Washington, D.C., for home, he read a draft of the Emancipation Proclamation to his cabinet.

Lincoln's draft poorly masked the radical content with legalism and gradualism. He claimed merely to be complying with congressional legislation requiring him to deliver an enacting order of the Militia Act and Second Confiscation Act. Further, he described emancipation as a "military measure" only, one not altering "the constitutional relation between the general government, and each, and all of the states."[10] Only those slaves in rebellious areas would be "forever free"—and not until January 1, 1863. States that abandoned the rebellion before that date would receive the same deal that Lincoln had given the Border States. They could hold on to slavery, or, if they wished, they could abolish it, gradually or immediately, and receive funds from Congress for compensation and colonization.

The president may have hoped that the Proclamation would seem moderate, but his cabinet saw it for what it was: a document that would change the nature of the war and set slavery on a sure path to destruction. Even the cabinet's most radical member, Salmon P. Chase, the secretary of the treasury, was taken aback. He recommended that Lincoln instead authorize each military commander to issue his own distinct proclamation. All the cabinet members shared Secretary of State William H. Seward's concern that the Proclamation might look like an act of desperation by a nearly defeated Union. Yet they acceded to Lincoln's wish to issue the order, while Lincoln yielded to Seward's point about the Proclamation appearing as a "last *shriek*, on the retreat," and agreed not to deliver the Proclamation until the Union had a military victory.[11] He would have to wait two months.

Poised to deliver the Proclamation, Lincoln now pushed harder for the gradualist measures he wanted attached to emancipation: compensation and colonization. In the annual message that he was preparing to send to Congress in December, he recommended constitutional amendments providing funds to compensate loyal slaveowners and to colonize ex-slaves abroad. He also recommended specific plans of colonization. First, he approved of a scheme of settlement in Chiriquí, in what is now Panama. But he abandoned that location when it became clear that it would violate treaty obligations with European nations. Later, he contracted with the owner of a small island near Haiti, Île à Vache, to send freed people there.

Knowing that the success of colonization depended on African Americans' willingness to resettle, Lincoln invited local free black leaders, most of them ministers, to the White House to sell them on the idea. The *New York Tribune* published the only record of the meeting. Assuming that the transcript is accurate, the president was uncharacteristically tactless, even insulting, that day. "You and we . . . have between us a broader difference than exists between almost any other two races," he began. "I think your race suffer very greatly, many of them by living among us, while ours suffer from your presence. In a word we suffer on each side. If this is admitted, it affords a reason at least why we should be separated." Then, meaning to attribute the war to the institution of slavery, he seemed instead to blame it on the slaves themselves and on free African Americans as well. "But for your race among us there could not be war," he told his visitors, "although many men engaged on either side do not care for you one way or the other." After presenting his scheme of colonizing blacks in Central America, he dismissed them, telling them he looked forward to their response.[12]

Most African Americans refused to go along with the president's plan. John S. Rock, a prominent black abolitionist, earlier that year had said that colonization was nothing but a scheme of "white people . . . to get rid of us." He had ridiculed the claim that colonization was a benevolent movement to care for those unready for freedom. "The free people of color have succeeded, in spite of every effort to crush them," Rock had declared, "and we are to-day a living refutation of that shameless assertion that we 'can't take care of ourselves' in a state of freedom."[13] Even those African Americans who agreed to settle abroad did so with reluctance and resentment. In April 1862, at about the time that Congress abolished slavery in Washington, D.C., a group of nearly sixty African Americans from the District petitioned Congress to be colonized in Central America. Beneath their pleading and respectful tone was condemnation of a country that regarded them as "evil" and "debarred [them] from rights of citizenship," even though their hearts clung "to the land of our birth."[14] Lincoln's speech to the delegation at the White House did little to convert African Americans to the colonization cause. Indeed, it may have turned many against it. In reaction to the speech, the abolitionist Frederick Douglass condemned Lincoln for "his contempt for negroes and his canting hypocrisy." "Mr. Lincoln is quite a genuine representative of American prejudices and negro hatred," Douglass wrote. He was, Douglass added, "far more concerned for the preservation of slavery, and the favor of the Border Slave States, than for any sentiment of magnanimity or principle of justice and humanity."[15]

As Lincoln moved forward on colonization, he also prepared to defend the Proclamation against public criticism. To Horace Greeley, the editor of the *New York Tribune*, who had published a plea for Lincoln to free the slaves, Lincoln wrote a public letter saying that he would act against slavery only if it helped preserve the Union. The "paramount object in this struggle *is* to save the Union," he declared, "and is *not* either to save or to destroy slavery" (Document 14). Yet defending emancipation as a means to save the Union met only one sort of objection. Even if emancipation was the right course, what gave the president the power to issue such an order? Lincoln adopted John Quincy Adams's old idea that the Constitution authorized extraordinary measures, even emancipation, in times of war. He had already claimed that the Constitution gave him "war powers" as commander in chief, such as the power to suspend the right of habeas corpus to civilians who interfered with military operations. Now he would use his war powers to free the slaves in rebellious areas.

Lincoln's wait for a Union military victory ended in mid-September 1862 with the Battle of Antietam (also known as Sharpsburg) in Maryland. Despite the unprecedented losses on both sides, Lincoln could declare the battle a victory because it ended a Confederate invasion. On September 22, he issued the preliminary Emancipation Proclamation (Document 15).

Lincoln's opponents, and even some of his allies, were outraged. Democrats in the North joined Confederates in denouncing Lincoln as a tyrant, an abolitionist devil, and even a reincarnation of John Brown. The editor of the *Cincinnati Daily Enquirer* pronounced, "The idea that twenty millions of Northerners can not conquer eight millions of Southern men, without calling in the assistance of negroes, and using servile insurrection as an instrument, can not be other wise than humiliating to American pride" (Document 23). For Benjamin R. Curtis, a leading jurist in the country—he had recently stepped down from the U.S. Supreme Court, where he had issued a dissent in the *Dred Scott* case—Lincoln had clearly overreached his authority in resting the Proclamation on the war powers of the presidency (Document 16). Democrats in the state elections in October and November successfully ran against the Proclamation. Although they took three new seats in the Senate, the Republicans were still well in control of the chamber. In the House of Representatives, however, the Democrats gained thirty-four seats, leaving the Republicans with only a slight majority. Pundits began to speculate that Lincoln might retreat by not issuing a final proclamation or by modifying the order.

Lincoln kept his promise, however. On January 1, 1863, he signed the final Emancipation Proclamation (Document 21). The document's longest section listed the areas excluded from the Proclamation, including most of those in the Confederacy occupied by Union troops. Also exempt were the western counties of Virginia, which would become the new state of West Virginia. Lincoln signed the act creating the state the day before he issued the final Proclamation. The admission of West Virginia, the constitution of which prohibited slavery, conformed to Lincoln's preference for emancipation by state action. Even after he issued the final Proclamation, Lincoln continued to argue that the war—even now that it was a war for emancipation—would not destroy the powers of the states. To one of his generals he wrote, "The States not included in it [the Proclamation] . . . can have their rights in the Union as of old. Even the people of the states included, if they choose, need not to be hurt by it."[16] The president continued to look to the Border States, which were left untouched by the Proclamation, to abolish slavery by state action, and he never broadened the scope of the Proclamation to include the Border States or other exempted areas.

Even so, the Emancipation Proclamation was a powerful document, and Lincoln knew it. He struggled with every word, making small but significant changes to the preliminary Proclamation. Gone was any promise of compensation to slaveowners. Colonization also disappeared, and Lincoln would never endorse it again—at least publicly. Instead, the Emancipation Proclamation authorized the recruitment of former slaves into the armed services, although it did not explicitly say that blacks could serve in combat. Lincoln knew that many white Americans feared that putting armed ex-slaves into the field would start a race war. European officials shared those concerns: A slave rebellion might destroy the cotton that supplied European mills. So Lincoln replaced a phrase in the preliminary Proclamation approving of slaves taking steps toward their own liberation with one asking them "to abstain from all violence, unless in necessary self-defence," and suggesting that "they labor faithfully for reasonable wages." Although the Proclamation did not authorize combat service for African Americans, within a few months the president would oversee the creation of the Bureau of Colored Troops, which organized black regiments to fight against Confederates. Almost 200,000 African American men eventually served in the Union army and navy. One other feature distinguished the final Proclamation from the preliminary one. Although it followed the preliminary Proclamation in couching emancipation in terms of military necessity, it ended with an unequivocal moral statement: The Proclamation was "an act of justice," which, Lincoln hoped, would receive "the gracious favor of Almighty God."

The Emancipation Proclamation may have been dry in its wording—Karl Marx, who was working as a newspaper correspondent in London at the time, likened it to "ordinary summonses sent by one lawyer to another on the opposing side"—but in setting millions of humans "forever free," the document had a world-shaking power beyond anything that Marx would ever compose.[17] It transformed the Civil War from a war only for Union to a war for Union *and* emancipation. It dashed Confederates' hopes that European nations, particularly England and France, would join them as allies. How could these nations, which had already abolished slavery, wage war against the cause of emancipation? Finally, in invoking God's will for emancipation, the Proclamation gave the war a noble, even a holy, purpose.

THE PROMISE OF EMANCIPATION

Did the Emancipation Proclamation set anyone free? The question, often asked, is unanswerable in any meaningful way. It was one step among many that led to African American liberation. But it was a crucial step. In declaring black liberation a war aim, Lincoln's words pushed the United States far forward in the struggle to end slavery. Yet in that struggle, as Lincoln knew, arms would be as decisive as words.

African Americans, who had helped force emancipation to the surface as a war aim, also knew the significance of helping the Union war effort, which not only ensured emancipation but also held out the possibility of legal equality. Even before the Emancipation Proclamation, Congress had authorized the creation of a few black regiments; the Proclamation merely opened the floodgates of black recruits. Three months after Lincoln signed the document, Frederick Douglass rallied African Americans to fight, telling them that "liberty won by white men would lack half its lustre" (Document 28). Regardless of what the Proclamation did or did not do, African Americans saw and seized the opportunity to struggle for their own freedom.

Just as the rewards could be greater for African Americans serving in combat, so were the risks. Black soldiers were subject to racism in the ranks and from civilians. During the New York City draft riots of July 1863, rioters targeted African Americans in uniform. Black soldiers were humiliated by policies that restricted them from command and paid them less than white soldiers, at least at first. Worst of all, they put their lives at risk in a way that white soldiers could hardly imagine: If their former owners learned that they had joined the Union army, they might take out their rage on family members still enslaved. If Confederate soldiers captured them, they were to be turned over to state authorities, who might return them to their owners or execute them as slaves in rebellion. Lincoln reacted to this policy by declaring that one Confederate prisoner would be killed for every Union soldier executed. Lincoln's order had little effect in practice, as southern authorities usually returned captured African Americans to their previous owners or tried to exchange them for Confederate prisoners. But the order nonetheless was powerful in its egalitarian message. African Americans deserved an equal share of the honor due to all soldiers. When a conservative counseled Lincoln to retract or modify the Emancipation Proclamation, he responded that if black soldiers "stake their lives for us they must be prompted by the strongest motive—even the promise of freedom. And the promise being made, must be kept."[18]

Yet what exactly was the promise of freedom? Freedom might be promised to African American soldiers, but what about black civilians, especially those in areas not covered by the Emancipation Proclamation? More than a year after he signed the Proclamation, Lincoln received a letter from a Maryland slave named Annie Davis, who asked if she was allowed to leave her white female owner and travel to see her family on the state's Eastern Shore. "You will please let me know if we are free," she wrote to Lincoln, "and what I can do" (Document 44). Luckily for Davis, Maryland voted to abolish slavery later in 1864. Missouri, which had passed an act of gradual emancipation in 1863, enacted a new law in early 1865 abolishing slavery immediately. Congress did what it could. In early 1865, it extended the promise of the 1862 Militia Act by freeing the wives and children of black soldiers everywhere, not just in areas in rebellion. At the same time, Congress created the Freedmen's Bureau to help oversee African Americans' transition from slaves to free laborers. But the laws could not by themselves keep masters from abusing the enslaved family members of black soldiers. These soldiers and their white allies would sometimes take matters into their own hands. Readying himself for his march to the Missouri town where his family and former master lived, the black soldier Spotswood Rice wrote to the woman who now owned his children, "I will have . . . powrer and autherity . . . to exacute vengencens on them that holds my Child" (Document 34). For northern African Americans as well, the Emancipation Proclamation may have signaled a shift in race relations, but actual change would take time and further struggle. African Americans in northern cities were still excluded from most white schools, streetcars, hotels, and restaurants, and very few African Americans enjoyed the right to vote. For African Americans determined to see an end to segregation and discrimination, the Emancipation Proclamation carried the promise that the words *black* and *white* would disappear from state laws, city codes, and private charters, leaving all Americans, regardless of color, equal in the eyes of God, the law, and the marketplace.

As Lincoln himself often admitted, the Emancipation Proclamation did not guarantee blacks freedom, much less legal equality. The U.S. Supreme Court might rule that the Proclamation had no effect beyond the war. Or, more likely, Lincoln might lose the election of 1864, in which case his successor could negotiate emancipation away. Fearing that slavery might somehow survive the war, antislavery activists and lawmakers moved quickly to put emancipation on surer footing. In April 1864, the Senate adopted a resolution for an antislavery constitutional amendment by the requisite two-thirds majority. But the House of Representatives did not have the votes to carry the measure, and the vote there fell short in June 1864.

Meanwhile, although Lincoln listened to his advisers who suggested modifying or retracting the Proclamation to curry favor with conservatives, whose votes he needed in the upcoming presidential election, he held fast to emancipation. He made sure that the proposed constitutional amendment abolishing slavery appeared in his party's national campaign platform, and he wrote a letter that appeared in all Union newspapers declaring that union *and* emancipation had to be preconditions to any peace negotiations with the Confederacy. Even when, in late August, the president became convinced that he would lose the election, he refused to backpedal on emancipation. Union military victories that fall, especially the capture of Atlanta by General William T. Sherman, helped carry the election for Lincoln. Had George B. McClellan, the Democratic candidate, won the election instead of Lincoln, he might well have removed emancipation as a precondition for peace. With Lincoln reelected, emancipation rested on a surer footing.

Once the election was over, Lincoln wasted no time in pressing the House of Representatives to reconsider the antislavery amendment. He even buttonholed a few congressmen who had opposed the measure to ask that they change their votes. Enough of those who had voted against the measure in the previous session changed their position or sat out the final vote so that the resolution for the amendment was adopted by Congress on January 31, 1865, and sent to the states for ratification.

By the time Congress had approved the amendment, the Confederacy had taken its own steps toward emancipation to meet its desperate need for soldiers. At the beginning of the war, some white southerners had made the argument that a small number of slaves could be freed and put into Confederate uniform without dissolving slavery as the cornerstone of the Confederacy. As proof, they pointed to the free African Americans who had formed a Confederate regiment called the Louisiana Native Guards at the start of the war. The Union's emancipation policy had persuaded African Americans that their interests lay with the United States, not the Confederacy. A number of those who had served in the Native Guards now served in a regiment of the same name that fought for the Union. But it was not too late, some Confederate leaders began arguing in 1864, to bring the slaves into their ranks. Confederate general Patrick R. Cleburne led a group of western commanders in pleading with the Confederate government to begin emancipating and recruiting African Americans (Document 35). President Jefferson Davis ordered all such talk to cease. But by early 1865, the logic of Confederate emancipation was almost inescapable. The Union army had taken Atlanta, Savannah, and Mobile Bay and was poised to capture Richmond. There were almost as many African Americans in Union uniform as there were white soldiers in all the Confederate armed forces. To rally sagging southern spirits, Davis delivered a number of speeches reminding his constituents that they were fighting for an independent nation free from northern tyranny, not simply the possession of black people as slaves. It was a small step for Davis and other Confederate leaders to reason that if freeing and arming some of those slaves would aid the cause of

Confederate independence, southern whites could not oppose the move. Even the South's military hero, Robert E. Lee, supported the proposal.

Yet, when Davis proposed such a measure, southern whites balked. The editor of the *Charleston Mercury* sneered, "The soldiers of South Carolina will not fight beside a nigger" (Document 38). The Confederate Congress failed to carry a measure freeing slaves and recruiting them into the military. Instead, it merely authorized states to take these steps. No state acted except Virginia, which in the spring of 1865 recruited a few dozen African American men into regiments on the promise that they would be free. The move came too late. On April 9, 1865, General Lee surrendered the Army of Northern Virginia to General Ulysses S. Grant. Yet these small steps toward emancipation in Virginia, the site of the insurrections of Nat Turner and John Brown, revealed how much things had changed in such a short time.

Abraham Lincoln, who believed—rightly—that his greatest legacy would be the Emancipation Proclamation, did not live to see emancipation become law. On April 14, 1865, he was shot by John Wilkes Booth. He died early the next day. Antislavery politicians invoked the name of their latest martyr as they pushed the state legislatures to ratify the constitutional amendment abolishing slavery. The new president, Andrew Johnson, followed Lincoln's lead in accepting ratifications from new Unionist legislatures in states that had seceded. On December 18, 1865, Secretary of State Seward announced that the amendment had been ratified. Freedom, not slavery, was now the nation's cornerstone.

THE CONTESTED MEMORY OF EMANCIPATION

Even after the Thirteenth Amendment abolishing slavery was adopted, the Emancipation Proclamation was the document most associated with the end of slavery in the United States, and its author, Abraham Lincoln, was most often credited with emancipation. Southern whites who refused to accept defeat denounced Lincoln and the Proclamation. But outside of those nostalgic for the noble "lost cause" of the Confederacy, Americans tended to single out the Emancipation Proclamation as the defining document of the Civil War. The painting by Francis Carpenter of Lincoln reading the Emancipation Proclamation to his cabinet quickly became an icon. During Reconstruction, Republican politicians drew a direct line from the Emancipation Proclamation to the Fourteenth Amendment, ratified in 1868, which granted citizenship and equal rights to African Americans, and to the Fifteenth Amendment, ratified in 1870, which guaranteed voting rights to African American men. (Another fifty years would pass before women of all races would secure the ballot.) Framed portraits of Lincoln and reprints of the Emancipation Proclamation decorated African American homes like religious art.

Beginning in the last decades of the nineteenth century, however, the Emancipation Proclamation began to lose its luster and even to recede from public memory. Within a decade of the end of the Civil War, much of what African Americans had associated with freedom lay far from their reach. The federal government stood idly by or even cooperated as southern whites reclaimed land that had been promised to freed blacks. And although the Union army had at first enforced Reconstruction policies and protected the newly won civil and political rights of African Americans, only a small number of troops remained in the South. By the end of 1877, all the troops were gone, and all the southern states were ruled by white governments willing to turn a blind eye to the violence and disfranchisement visited upon black communities. In such a climate, it was difficult for African Americans to praise Lincoln and the Emancipation Proclamation unconditionally. Frederick Douglass gave voice to their ambivalence in a speech on April 14, 1876, the year of the nation's centennial, although the timing was coincidental. The occasion was the dedication of the Freedmen's Memorial in Washington, D.C., on the eleventh anniversary of Lincoln's assassination. The memorial featured a statue of the heroic Lincoln standing above a kneeling slave in chains (Document 49). Douglass was dismayed by the submissive pose of the slave. He praised Lincoln, whom he had genuinely viewed as a friend, but he also reminded his audience that "viewed from the genuine abolition ground, Mr. Lincoln seemed tardy, cold, dull, and indifferent" (Document 48).

African American resentment played less of a role than whites' desire for national reconciliation in driving the Emancipation Proclamation from its place as the document most associated with the Civil War. In the last decades of the nineteenth century, as whites in the North and South tried to put the bitterness of the war behind them, they searched for a speech or document that could rally former enemies toward reconciliation. The Emancipation Proclamation would not do. It reminded southerners of the shame of slavery and northerners of the aggressiveness of war. It also projected Lincoln, now a world-renowned hero, as a northern rather than a national president. Much better for the purposes of reconciliation was the Gettysburg Address (Document 43), which Lincoln had delivered ten months after signing the Emancipation Proclamation. That document was more concise and poetic than the

Proclamation. It had no whiff of sectionalism and no mention of slavery. The "new birth of freedom" it proclaimed was for all Americans, not slaves alone. Americans had begun to recognize the beauty and power of the Gettysburg Address from the moment that Lincoln had delivered it, but only at the end of the nineteenth century did it eclipse the Emancipation Proclamation as the defining document of the Civil War. It was not that Americans had suddenly discovered the Gettysburg Address, but rather that a majority of them, mostly white, had discovered that it served their nationalist purposes better than the Emancipation Proclamation. Not until the 1960s, when the civil rights movement brought African Americans the justice that the Emancipation Proclamation had promised them, did it again compete with the Gettysburg Address as the sacred text of the war.[19]

In the last decades of the twentieth century, debate turned away from the question of whether emancipation was the central event of the Civil War—most historians agreed that it was—and toward the question of who or what was most responsible for emancipation. The debate was not new. In the early part of the century, as mainstream historians held up Lincoln as "the Great Emancipator," a few, such as the scholar and activist W. E. B. DuBois, criticized Lincoln's approach to black freedom as pragmatic rather than moral. DuBois emphasized instead the steps taken toward emancipation by the slaves themselves. Beginning in the late 1960s, historians clashed more visibly in a full-throated debate over Lincoln's role in emancipation. Helping to incite the debate was an article by the journalist Lerone Bennett Jr. titled "Was Abe Lincoln a White Supremacist?"[20] More than forty years after Bennett's article, the issue of Lincoln's role in African Americans' struggle for freedom and equality remains as contentious as ever. Particularly among social historians—those committed to understanding history more as the product of ordinary people than political leaders—emancipation has come to be understood as the consequence of the actions of slaves and free African Americans instead of the result of the efforts of Lincoln.

The recent debate over the origins and meaning of emancipation is as fascinating as the events surrounding emancipation, and both subjects—the making of emancipation and the struggle over its meaning—are central to this book. For this reason, no one person or group stands at the center of the book. Although there are more documents penned by Lincoln than by anyone else in this volume, these lie alongside reports about slaves, speeches by white and black abolitionists, northern and southern newspaper editorials reacting to emancipation, and essays by historians making competing claims about who deserves the most credit for black freedom. The purpose of this volume, then, is not to make the case for one actor being more responsible for emancipation than all others, but rather to reveal the rich complexity of the momentous process by which millions of African Americans, in a very short time and in the midst of the most violent conflict ever fought on American soil, became free.

NOTES

[1] Richard Hofstadter, *The American Political Tradition and the Men Who Made It* (1948; repr., New York: Vintage Books, 1973), 169.

[2] James G. Randall, *Constitutional Problems under Lincoln* (New York: D. Appleton, 1926), 374–76.

[3] Emerson, quoted in James M. McPherson, *Battle Cry of Freedom: The Civil War Era* (New York: Oxford University Press, 1988), 51.

[4] *Dred Scott v. John F. A. Sandford*, 60 U.S. 407 (1857).

[5] Roy P. Basler, ed., and Marion Dolores Pratt and Lloyd A. Dunlap, asst. eds., *The Collected Works of Abraham Lincoln* (New Brunswick, N.J.: Rutgers University Press, 1953–1955), 2:401.

[6] From *War of the Rebellion: A Compilation of the Official Records of the Union and Confederate Armies* (Washington, D.C.: Government Printing Office, 1894), ser. 2, 1:750.

[7] Michael Vorenberg, "Abraham Lincoln and the Politics of Black Colonization," *Journal of the Abraham Lincoln Association* 14 (Summer 1993): 23–46.

[8] Basler, *The Collected Works of Abraham Lincoln*, 5:222.

[9] Ibid., 5:317–18.

[10] Ibid., 5:336–37.

[11] Francis B. Carpenter, *Six Months at the White House with Abraham Lincoln* (New York: Hurd and Houghton, 1866), 22.

[12] Abraham Lincoln, "Address on Colonization to a Deputation of Negroes," August 14, 1862, in Basler, *The Collected Works of Abraham Lincoln*, 5:370–75.

[13] John Rock, "Speech, Annual Meeting of the Massachusetts Anti-Slavery Society, January 28, 1862," in *Liberator*, February 14, 1862.

[14] Joseph Enoch Williams et al., "Memorial," n.d. [April 1862], RG 233, ser. 467, Select Committee on Emancipation, Petitions and Memorials, House of Representatives, 37th Congress, box 88, folder HR 37A-G21.4, National Archives, Washington, D.C.

[15] Frederick Douglass, "The President and His Speeches," *Douglass' Monthly*, September 1862, 707–8.

[16] Abraham Lincoln to John A. McClernand, January 8, 1863, in Basler, *The Collected Works of Abraham Lincoln*, 6:49.

[17] Marx, quoted in Allen C. Guelzo, *Lincoln's Emancipation Proclamation: The End of Slavery in America* (New York: Simon & Schuster, 2004), 1.

[18] Abraham Lincoln to James C. Conkling, August 26, 1863, in Basler, *The Collected Works of Abraham Lincoln*, 6:409.

[19] Gabor S. Boritt, *The Gettysburg Gospel: The Lincoln Speech That Nobody Knows* (New York: Simon & Schuster, 2006), 175–94.

[20] Lerone Bennett Jr., "Was Abe Lincoln a White Supremacist?" *Ebony*, February 1968, 35–42. See also Arthur Zilversmit, "Lincoln and the Problem of Race: A Decade of Interpretations," *Papers of the Abraham Lincoln Association*, 2 (1980): 22–45.

PART TWO

The Documents

1

The Problem of Slavery at the Start of the Civil War

The presidential election of 1860 promised to be one of the most divisive and decisive in history. On the Democratic side, the leading contender was Senator Stephen A. Douglas of Illinois. As the primary architect of both the Compromise of 1850, which included the powerful new Fugitive Slave Law, and the Kansas-Nebraska Act of 1854, which potentially allowed slavery to exist in territories where it had been prohibited by the Missouri Compromise of 1820, Douglas was a northerner who respected the slaveholding rights of southerners. His solution to the problem of whether slavery should be allowed to expand westward was "popular sovereignty," which gave the people of a new territory or state the power to allow or prohibit slavery. That principle led to battles between proslavery and antislavery settlers in Kansas, which was admitted as a territory as a result of the Kansas-Nebraska Act. "Bleeding Kansas" became a struggle not only for the future of slavery in Kansas but also for the principle of slaveowning throughout the West. Proslavery forces ultimately won the conflict—or seemed to. A proslavery state constitution, known as the "Lecompton constitution" after the town in Kansas where it was crafted, was officially approved by voters in 1858, though the election was marred by fraud. President James Buchanan ignored the obvious irregularities of the election results and endorsed the constitution. Douglas opposed the constitution because the improper vote in his opinion violated the principle of popular sovereignty. As a result, southern proslavery Democrats turned against Douglas. They found support in the U.S. Supreme Court, which in its *Dred Scott* decision of 1857 declared that Congress had no power to prohibit slavery in a territory, thus making it impossible for Douglas's popular sovereignty to work. Douglas continued to insist that the people did have the right to prohibit slavery, even if by informal, local measures. By 1860, southern proslavery Democrats began to consider leaving the national party or at least backing another candidate.

 nile, the Republican Party, a relatively new organization that
:d in the wake of the Kansas-Nebraska Act and opposed the
of slavery, was uncertain who its presidential candidate would
be in 1860. One possibility was Abraham Lincoln, a one-term congressman from Illinois who had gained national fame in his well-publicized
run for the U.S. Senate against Stephen Douglas in 1858. Lincoln had
lost the race, but his debates with Douglas, which were published in
newspapers across the nation, helped establish his reputation as a
powerful orator who might be more electable than some other, more
renowned members of the party, especially William H. Seward. A U.S.
senator from New York, Seward was thought by many to be too radical
for the nomination after he delivered a famous 1858 speech suggesting an "irrepressible conflict" to come between slavery and free labor.
Looking toward the possible nomination, Lincoln accepted an invitation
to speak at New York's Cooper Union in February 1860 (Document 1).
That speech defined his candidacy. He was morally opposed to slavery
but would not interfere with it where it already existed — in the southern
states (Document 3). He asked only that it be prohibited from expand-
ing to the West (Document 2). Also moderate was his position on the
Fugitive Slave Law, which he accepted as it was. He admonished those
who interfered with the enforcement of the law, and he denounced violent abolitionists such as John Brown, who had risen to fame in Bleeding
Kansas during the mid-1850s and had raided the federal arsenal at Harpers Ferry, Virginia, in 1859 in an attempt to stir up a slave insurrection.
Lincoln's moral stance, combined with his moderate approach, won him
the Republican nomination. The Democratic Party then split along sectional lines, with northern Democrats nominating Stephen Douglas and
southern Democrats nominating John C. Breckinridge. A split Democratic vote helped Lincoln win both the popular vote and the electoral
college in the general election in November 1860.

Proslavery leaders in the South reacted with fury to the election.
They called the result antidemocratic. Lincoln had not received one
southern electoral vote, they pointed out, and he represented only the
North. Secession conventions took place in all of the Deep South states
soon after the election. South Carolina was the first to secede, in December 1860. In Georgia, a number of leaders, including the former Whig
congressman Alexander H. Stephens, cautioned against seceding until
Lincoln showed what he would actually do after taking office in March
1861 — or at least until a large enough group of southern states seceded
in cooperation with one another. Stephens lost the day: The Georgia
convention, of which he was a member, voted for secession in mid-
January 1861. Stephens remained loyal to his state and abided by the

vote. When the Confederate States of America was formed by the seven states that had seceded, Stephens was elected to the new Confederate Congress and then chosen as vice president of the Confederacy, serving under President Jefferson Davis. In March 1861, Stephens delivered his famous "Cornerstone Speech" (Document 5), which declared slavery the cornerstone of the Confederacy. The states of the upper South still followed the lead of the "Conditional Unionists," who pledged loyalty to the Union on the condition that the new president not take hostile action against the South or slavery.

By the time Lincoln delivered his First Inaugural on March 4, 1861 (Document 5), the Confederacy had existed for almost a month and had claimed possession of all U.S. property in the South, including federal forts such as Fort Moultrie and Fort Sumter in Charleston, South Carolina. From his election to the First Inaugural, Lincoln urged his fellow Republicans to remain steadfast in their commitment to containing slavery in the South, and he asked all Americans to hold fast to the Union.

1

ABRAHAM LINCOLN

Cooper Union Address

February 27, 1860

As Lincoln positioned himself to be a contender for the Republican presidential nomination, he distanced himself from radicals such as John Brown, while painting southern whites as the real extremists.

And now, if they would listen—as I suppose they will not—I would address a few words to the Southern people. . . .

You charge that we stir up insurrections among your slaves. We deny it; and what is your proof? Harper's Ferry! John Brown!! John Brown was no Republican; and you have failed to implicate a single Republican in his Harper's Ferry enterprise. . . .

From Roy P. Basler, ed., and Marion Dolores Pratt and Lloyd A. Dunlap, asst. eds., *The Collected Works of Abraham Lincoln* (New Brunswick, N.J.: Rutgers University Press, 1953–1955), 3:535, 537–43.

Republican doctrines and declarations are accompanied with a continual protest against any interference whatever with your slaves, or with you about your slaves. Surely, this does not encourage them to revolt. True, we do . . . declare our belief that slavery is wrong; but the slaves do not hear us declare even this. For anything we say or do, the slaves would scarcely know there is a Republican party. I believe they would not, in fact, generally know it but for your misrepresentations of us, in their hearing. In your political contests among yourselves, each faction charges the other with sympathy with Black Republicanism; and then, to give point to the charge, defines Black Republicanism to simply be insurrection, blood and thunder among the slaves.

Slave insurrections are no more common now than they were before the Republican party was organized. What induced the Southampton insurrection, twenty-eight years ago, in which, at least, three times as many lives were lost as at Harper's Ferry?[1] You can scarcely stretch your very elastic fancy to the conclusion that Southampton was "got up by Black Republicanism." In the present state of things in the United States, I do not think a general, or even a very extensive slave insurrection, is possible. The indispensable concert of action cannot be attained. The slaves have no means of rapid communication; nor can incendiary freemen, black or white, supply it. The explosive materials are everywhere in parcels; but there neither are, nor can be supplied, the indispensable connecting trains.

Much is said by Southern people about the affection of slaves for their masters and mistresses; and a part of it, at least, is true. A plot for an uprising could scarcely be devised and communicated to twenty individuals before some one of them, to save the life of a favorite master or mistress, would divulge it. . . .

John Brown's effort was peculiar. It was not a slave insurrection. It was an attempt by white men to get up a revolt among slaves, in which the slaves refused to participate. In fact, it was so absurd that the slaves, with all their ignorance, saw plainly enough it could not succeed. . . .

There is a judgment and a feeling against slavery in this nation, which cast at least a million and a half of votes. You cannot destroy that judgment and feeling—that sentiment—by breaking up the political organization which rallies around it. . . . You will break up the Union rather than submit to a denial of your Constitutional rights. . . .

---

[1] Lincoln here is referring to the Nat Turner revolt of 1831, in Southampton County, Virginia, in which the slave Turner and about fifty other enslaved and free African Americans killed almost sixty white men, women, and children.

That has a somewhat reckless sound; but it would be palliated, if not fully justified, were we proposing, by the mere force of numbers, to deprive you of some right, plainly written down in the Constitution. But we are proposing no such thing.

When you make these declarations, you have a specific and well-understood allusion to an assumed Constitutional right of yours, to take slaves into the federal territories, and to hold them there as property. But no such right is specifically written in the Constitution. That instrument is literally silent about any such right. We, on the contrary, deny that such a right has any existence in the Constitution, even by implication.

Your purpose, then, plainly stated, is, that you will destroy the Government, unless you be allowed to construe and enforce the Constitution as you please, on all points in dispute between you and us. You will rule or ruin in all events.

2

ABRAHAM LINCOLN

Letter to Lyman Trumbull

December 10, 1860

While he was president-elect, between the November 1860 election and the March 4, 1861, inauguration, Lincoln avoided making specific policy recommendations beyond those already articulated during the campaign. As politicians during this period considered various compromise measures, Lincoln wrote fellow Republicans, including Senator Lyman Trumbull from his home state of Illinois, urging them not to back down from the party's stance against popular sovereignty and all other measures that might allow slavery into the western territories.

From Roy P. Basler, ed., and Marion Dolores Pratt and Lloyd A. Dunlap, asst. eds., *The Collected Works of Abraham Lincoln* (New Brunswick, N.J.: Rutgers University Press, 1953–1955), 4:149–50.

My dear Sir:

Let there be no compromise on the question of *extending* slavery. If there be, all our labor is lost, and, ere long, must be done again. The dangerous ground—that into which some of our friends have a hankering to run—is Pop. Sov.[2] Have none of it. Stand firm. The tug has to come, & better now, than any time hereafter.

[2] Popular sovereignty.

3

ABRAHAM LINCOLN

Letter to Alexander H. Stephens

December 22, 1860

Alexander Hamilton Stephens, who was born in Georgia, was a long-time acquaintance of Abraham Lincoln. They were both Whigs, and they served in Congress together from 1847 to 1849. It was natural, then, that Lincoln turned to Stephens to deliver his reassuring message that the federal government would not interfere with slavery where it already existed.

I fully appreciate the present peril the country is in, and the weight of responsibility on me.

Do the people of the South really entertain fears that a Republican administration would, *directly,* or *indirectly,* interfere with their slaves, or with them, about their slaves? If they do, I wish to assure you, as once a friend, and still, I hope, not an enemy, that there is no cause for such fears.

The South would be in no more danger in this respect, than it was in the days of Washington. I suppose, however, this does not meet the case. You think slavery is *right* and ought to be extended; while we think it is *wrong* and ought to be restricted. That I suppose is the rub. It certainly is the only substantial difference between us.

From Roy P. Basler, ed., and Marion Dolores Pratt and Lloyd A. Dunlap, asst. eds., *The Collected Works of Abraham Lincoln* (New Brunswick, N.J.: Rutgers University Press, 1953–1955), 4:160.

4

ALEXANDER H. STEPHENS

Cornerstone Speech

March 21, 1861

On December 30, 1860, Stephens replied to Lincoln's message (Document 3) that he was indeed a friend, and he urged Lincoln to press for the survival of the Union through public statements against radicalism. Less than a month later, Georgia seceded from the Union, and Stephens reversed his position. A month after assuming the vice presidency of the Confederacy, in February 1861, Stephens delivered his "Cornerstone Speech" in Savannah, Georgia. Some reporters took down the speech, but no original text survives. The text here was originally printed in the Savannah Republican *and was widely reprinted throughout the Confederacy and the Union. It soon became the best-known example of a racial justification for slavery and the creation of the Confederacy.*

We are passing through one of the greatest revolutions in the annals of the world. Seven States have within the last three months thrown off an old government and formed a new. This revolution has been signally marked, up to this time, by the fact of its having been accomplished without the loss of a single drop of blood. . . .

The new [Confederate] constitution has put at rest, *forever*, all the agitating questions relating to our peculiar institution—African slavery as it exists amongst us—the proper *status* of the negro in our form of civilization. This was the immediate cause of the late rupture and present revolution. Jefferson in his forecast, had anticipated this, as the "rock upon which the old Union would split." He was right. What was conjecture with him, is now a realized fact. But whether he fully comprehended the great truth upon which that rock *stood* and *stands*, may be doubted. The prevailing ideas entertained by him and most of the leading statesmen at the time of the formation of the old constitution, were that the enslavement of the African was in violation of the laws of

---

From Henry Cleveland, ed., *Alexander H. Stephens, in Public and Private, with Letters and Speeches, before, during, and since the War* (Philadelphia: National Publishing, 1866), 718, 721–23.

nature; that it was wrong in *principle*, socially, morally, and politically. . . . Those ideas, however, were fundamentally wrong. They rested upon the assumption of the equality of races. This was an error. It was a sandy foundation, and the government built upon it fell. . . .

Our new government is founded upon exactly the opposite idea; its foundations are laid, its corner-stone rests upon the great truth, that the negro is not equal to the white man; that slavery—subordination to the superior race—is his natural and normal condition. [Applause.]

This, our new government, is the first, in the history of the world, based upon this great physical, philosophical, and moral truth. This truth has been slow in the process of its development, like all other truths in the various departments of science. It has been so even amongst us. Many who hear me, perhaps, can recollect well, that this truth was not generally admitted, even within their day. The errors of the past generation still clung to many as late as twenty years ago. Those at the North, who still cling to these errors, with a zeal above knowledge, we justly denominate fanatics. . . . They assume that the negro is equal, and hence conclude that he is entitled to equal privileges and rights with the white man. . . .

[The Confederacy] is the first government ever instituted upon the principles in strict conformity to nature, and the ordination of Providence, in furnishing the materials of human society. Many governments have been founded upon the principle of the subordination and serfdom of certain classes of the same race; such were and are in violation of the laws of nature. Our system commits no such violation of nature's laws. With us, all of the white race, however high or low, rich or poor, are equal in the eye of the law. Not so with the negro. Subordination is his place. He, by nature, or by the curse against Canaan,[3] is fitted for that condition which he occupies in our system. . . .

It is, indeed, in conformity with the ordinance of the Creator. It is not for us to inquire into the wisdom of his ordinances, or to question them. For his own purposes, he has made one race to differ from another, as he has made "one star to differ from another star in glory."

The great objects of humanity are best attained when there is conformity to his laws and decrees, in the formation of governments as well as in all things else. Our confederacy is founded upon principles in strict conformity with these laws. This stone which was rejected by the first builders "is become the chief of the corner"—the real "cornerstone"—in our new edifice. [Applause.]

---

[3] In the Bible (Gen. 9:20–27), God curses Canaan, son of Ham, making him a slave. Many proslavery writers argued that blacks were the descendants of Ham and Canaan and that the biblical passage justified their enslavement.

5

ABRAHAM LINCOLN

First Inaugural

March 4, 1861

Lincoln faced a number of crises when he delivered his First Inaugural. Seven states of the Deep South had seceded and formed the Confederacy. Lincoln denied the legitimacy of secession and the new southern nation. In the early parts of his speech, he upheld both the ideal of Union and the laws protecting slavery, including the Fugitive Slave Law of 1850. He then denounced secession as unconstitutional and a form of "anarchy." Finally, as proof of his commitment not to touch slavery where it existed, he endorsed a resolution recently passed by Congress for a constitutional amendment that would prohibit federal interference with slavery in the southern states and that could never be altered or repealed. The measure, sometimes called the "first Thirteenth Amendment" (as opposed to the actual Thirteenth Amendment, which abolished slavery and was ratified in 1865), was ratified by only a few states.

Apprehension seems to exist among the people of the Southern States, that by the accession of a Republican Administration, their property, and their peace, and personal security, are to be endangered. There has never been any reasonable cause for such apprehension. Indeed, the most ample evidence to the contrary has all the while existed, and been open to their inspection. It is found in nearly all the published speeches of him who now addresses you. I do but quote from one of those speeches when I declare that "I have no purpose, directly or indirectly, to interfere with the institution of slavery in the States where it exists. I believe I have no lawful right to do so, and I have no inclination to do so." Those who nominated and elected me did so with full knowledge that I had made this, and many similar declarations, and had never recanted them. And more than this, they placed in the platform, for my acceptance, and as a law to themselves, and to me, the clear and emphatic resolution which I now read:

From Roy P. Basler, ed., and Marion Dolores Pratt and Lloyd A. Dunlap, asst. eds., *The Collected Works of Abraham Lincoln* (New Brunswick, N.J.: Rutgers University Press, 1953–1955), 4:262–63, 265–66, 268–71.

"*Resolved,* That the maintenance inviolate of the rights of the States, and especially the right of each State to order and control its own domestic institutions according to its own judgment exclusively, is essential to that balance of power on which the perfection and endurance of our political fabric depend; and we denounce the lawless invasion by armed force of the soil of any State or Territory, no matter under what pretext, as among the gravest of crimes." . . .

It follows . . . that no State, upon its own mere motion, can lawfully get out of the Union,—that *resolves* and *ordinances* to that effect are legally void; and that acts of violence, within any State or States, against the authority of the United States, are insurrectionary or revolutionary, according to circumstances.

I therefore consider that, in view of the Constitution and the laws, the Union is unbroken; and, to the extent of my ability, I shall take care, as the Constitution itself expressly enjoins upon me, that the laws of the Union be faithfully executed in all the States. Doing this I deem to be only a simple duty on my part; and I shall perform it, so far as practicable, unless my rightful masters, the American people, shall withhold the requisite means, or, in some authoritative manner, direct the contrary. I trust this will not be regarded as a menace, but only as the declared purpose of the Union that it *will* constitutionally defend, and maintain itself. . . .

One section of our country believes slavery is *right*, and ought to be extended, while the other believes it is *wrong*, and ought not to be extended. This is the only substantial dispute. . . .

Physically speaking, we cannot separate. We cannot remove our respective sections from each other, nor build an impassable wall between them. A husband and wife may be divorced, and go out of the presence, and beyond the reach of each other; but the different parts of our country cannot do this. They cannot but remain face to face; and intercourse, either amicable or hostile, must continue between them. . . .

I understand a proposed amendment to the Constitution—which amendment, however, I have not seen, has passed Congress, to the effect that the federal government, shall never interfere with the domestic institutions of the States, including that of persons held to service. . . . Holding such a provision to now be implied constitutional law, I have no objection to its being made express, and irrevocable. . . .

In *your* hands, my dissatisfied fellow countrymen, and not in *mine*, is the momentous issue of civil war. The government will not assail *you*. You can have no conflict, without being yourselves the aggressors. *You* have no oath registered in Heaven to destroy the government, while *I* shall have the most solemn one to "preserve, protect and defend" it.

I am loth to close. We are not enemies, but friends. We must not be enemies. Though passion may have strained, it must not break our bonds of affection. The mystic chords of memory, streching [*sic*] from every battle-field, and patriot grave, to every living heart and hearth-stone, all over this broad land, will yet swell the chorus of the Union, when again touched, as surely they will be, by the better angels of our nature.

2

The Impact of the Civil War on Slavery

In the early morning of April 12, 1861, as Union ships approached Charleston Harbor with troops and supplies on board, Confederate troops opened fire on Fort Sumter. The Union garrison there surrendered the next day. Lincoln called for seventy-five thousand volunteers to put down the rebellion, a move that helped trigger the secession of Arkansas, North Carolina, Tennessee, and Virginia, all of which joined the Confederate States of America. Richmond, Virginia, became the new capital of the Confederacy, and General Robert E. Lee, who turned down an offer to command all U.S. armed forces, accepted a position as a military adviser to President Jefferson Davis. In June 1862, Lee became commander of the eastern forces of the Confederacy, which he named the Army of Northern Virginia. The Confederates' strategy was primarily defensive. They sought to wear down Union morale until they secured Confederate independence. To demoralize northerners, Confederate troops also occasionally invaded Union territory with the hope of capturing or at least harassing Washington, D.C. Union troops at first sought to capture Richmond, an effort that in July 1861 resulted in the First Battle of Bull Run (or Manassas), a disaster for the Union army. After the battle, Lincoln appointed General George B. McClellan commander of the Army of the Potomac, the Union's army in the East. As McClellan enlarged and trained his army, other Union military forces sought to put a stranglehold on the Confederacy. The Union navy blockaded southern ports and sought to capture strategic Confederate harbors—most notably Charleston and New Orleans. Charleston held strong until the end of the war, but beginning in late 1861, Union forces were able to occupy much of the low country and the Sea Islands between Charleston and Savannah, Georgia. By the spring of 1862, Union forces had captured New Orleans, and Union troops began to occupy much of southeastern Louisiana. The key to the Union strategy of strangling the Confederacy was the Mississippi River, which Union gunboats sought to control so that Union troops could occupy the Mississippi Valley.

Even before the outbreak of the war, and certainly after it began, slavery and emancipation were central to the conflict. Some slaves, assuming that Lincoln's election and the onset of fighting signaled emancipation, escaped to Union forts and encampments. Their presence created tension between those Union troops who thought slaves should be returned to their owners—that was the official Union policy, and the Fugitive Slave Law of 1850 was still in effect—and those who thought they should be emancipated (Documents 7, 8, and 9). Many slaves found themselves closer to Union lines than they might otherwise have been, for some slaveowning Confederate soldiers brought their slaves with them to encampments. The Confederacy also purchased or conscripted hundreds of slaves to do the drudge work of the army. Slaves built forts and latrines, cooked and cleaned, tended to animals, and buried the dead. Some white southerners, such as John J. Cheatham of Georgia, thought that slaves should even be used in combat (Document 6). As the war continued, contact between slaves and Union forces increased, especially after Union armies occupied northern Virginia, the low country of South Carolina and Georgia, and parts of the Mississippi Valley. Enslaved African Americans faced difficult choices about how to respond to the conflict, and white soldiers and civilian officials struggled with the prospect of emancipation (Documents 10 and 11).

6

JOHN J. CHEATHAM

Letter to L. P. Walker

May 4, 1861

Less than a month after the firing on Fort Sumter, John J. Cheatham of Athens, Georgia, wrote to LeRoy Pope Walker, the Confederate secretary of war, predicting that Lincoln would free the slaves. Cheatham's remedy—to use slaves as soldiers in Confederate armies—was an unusual suggestion, which would not be taken up seriously by Confederate leaders

From John J. Cheatham to L. P. Walker, May 4, 1861, RG 109, ser. 5, Letters Received by the Confederate Secretary of War, 1861–1865, file 605 (1861), National Archives, Washington, D.C.

for another three years. But it reflected the state of mind of many white southerners as they faced the prospect of a war that would drain white fighting men from farms and plantations and leave behind potentially rebellious slaves.

[I hope] that you will agree with me, that it is the duty of every good and loyal citizen of our Southern Confederacy, however humble his position … in these times of arbitrary and tyrannical menace and war, to do all that he can to aid … the best interest and honor of that Confederacy. . . .

Some of our people are fearful that when a large portion of our fighting men are taken from the country, that large numbers of negroes aided by emissaries will ransack portions of the country, kill numbers of our inhabitants, and make their way to the black republicans. There is no doubt but that numbers of them believe that Lincoln's intention is to set them all free. Then, to counteract this idea and make them assist in whipping the black republicans, which by the by would be the best thing that could be done, could they not be incorporated into our armies, say ten or twenty placed promiscuously in each company? In this way the number would be too small to do our army any injury, whilst they might be made quite efficient in battle, as there are a great many that I have no doubt would make good soldiers and would willingly go if they had a chance. They might be valued as you would a horse or other property, and let the government pay for them provided they was killed in battle, and it should be made known to them that if they distinguished themselves by good conduct in battle, they should be rewarded. Could some plan of this sort be thought expedient and carried out with propriety, it would certainly lessen the dangers at home, and increase our strength in the field and would I have but little doubt, be responded to by large numbers of our people in all the States.

7

BENJAMIN F. BUTLER

Letter to Winfield Scott
May 24, 1861

---

*Union commanders were under orders to abide by the Fugitive Slave
Law of 1850 and return slaves who came into the lines to their rightful owners. In May 1861, General Benjamin F. Butler, the commander
of Fortress Monroe, in northeastern Virginia, refused to return slaves
unless their owners swore allegiance to the Union. Other Union commanders began to follow Butler's example of holding escaped slaves as
"contraband." Lincoln allowed these actions in the seceded states but not
in the Union slave states, also known as the Border States: Delaware,
Maryland, Kentucky, and Missouri. Soon African Americans within
Union lines became known as "contrabands," although Butler did not
use the term in his letter explaining his actions to Union general in chief
Winfield Scott.*

On Thursday night [May 23, 1861], three negroes, field hands, belonging to Col. Charles Mallory, now in command of the secession forces in
this district, delivered themselves up to my picket guard, and [were] . . .
detained by him. I immediately gave personal attention to the matter,
and found satisfactory evidence that these men were about to be taken
to Carolina for the purpose of aiding the secession forces there; that two
of them left wives and children (one a free woman) here; that the other
had left his master from fear that he would be called upon to take part
in the rebel armies. Satisfied of these facts from cautious examination of
each of the negroes apart from the others, I determined for the present,
and until better advised, as these men were very serviceable, and I had
great need of labor in my quartermaster's department, to avail myself of
their services, and that I would send a receipt to Colonel Mallory that I
had so taken them, as I would for any other property of a private citizen
which the exigencies of the service seemed to require to be taken by

---

From *War of the Rebellion: The Official Records of the Union and Confederate Armies*
(Washington, D.C.: Government Printing Office, 1880), ser. 1, 2:649–50.

me, and especially property that was designed, adapted, and about to be used against the United States.

As this is but an individual instance in a course of policy which may be required to be pursued with regard to this species of property, I have detailed to the Lieutenant-General this case, and ask his direction. I am credibly informed that the negroes in this neighborhood are now being employed in the erection of batteries and other works by the rebels, which it would be nearly or quite impossible to construct without their labor. Shall they be allowed the use of this property against the United States, and we not be allowed its use in aid of the United States? . . .

Major Cary [of the active Virginia volunteers] . . . desired to know if I did not feel myself bound by my constitutional obligations to deliver up fugitives under the fugitive-slave act. To this I replied that the fugitive-slave act did not affect a foreign country, which Virginia claimed to be . . . [and] that in Maryland, a loyal State, fugitives from service had been returned, and that even now, although so much pressed by my necessities for the use of these men of Colonel Mallory's, yet if their master would come to the fort and take the oath of allegiance to the Constitution of the United States I would deliver the men up to him and endeavor to hire their services of him if he desired to part with them.

8

ABRAHAM LINCOLN

Letter to Orville H. Browning

September 22, 1861

On August 6, 1861, Congress lent authority to the military's "contraband" policy by passing the First Confiscation Act, which authorized the seizure and liberation of slaves used against Union forces in rebellious areas. General John C. Frémont, who commanded Union forces in the West, took matters a step further on August 30 by imposing martial law in the Union state of Missouri and declaring free all slaves there. Lincoln feared

From Roy P. Basler, ed., and Marion Dolores Pratt and Lloyd A. Dunlap, asst. eds., *The Collected Works of Abraham Lincoln* (New Brunswick, N.J.: Rutgers University Press, 1953–1955), 4:531–32.

that Frémont's actions would turn Missouri and the other Border States against the Union, and he ordered the general to modify the proclamation so that the slaves were not emancipated. When Frémont refused, Lincoln overturned the proclamation. The president explained his reasoning to Orville H. Browning, a Republican who had been appointed to the U.S. Senate to fill the seat of Stephen A. Douglas, who died on June 3, 1861. Ten days after writing to Browning, Lincoln removed Frémont from command in Missouri and eventually reassigned him to the Mountain Department of western Virginia and eastern Tennessee.

Genl. Fremont's proclamation, as to confiscation of property, and the liberation of slaves, is *purely political*, and not within the range of *military* law, or necessity. If a commanding General finds a necessity to seize the farm of a private owner, for a pasture, an encampment, or a fortification, he has the right to do so, and to so hold it, as long as the necessity lasts; and this is within military law, because within military necessity. But to say the farm shall no longer belong to the owner, or his heirs forever; and this as well when the farm is not needed for military purposes as when it is, is purely political, without the savor of military law about it. And the same is true of slaves. If the General needs them, he can seize them, and use them; but when the need is past, it is not for him to fix their permanent future condition. That must be settled according to laws made by law-makers, and not by military proclamations. The proclamation in the point in question, is simply "dictatorship." It assumes that the general may do *anything* he pleases—confiscate the lands and free the slaves of *loyal* people, as well as of disloyal ones. . . . But I cannot assume this reckless position; nor allow others to assume it on my responsibility. You speak of it as being the only means of *saving* the government. On the contrary it is itself the surrender of the government. Can it be pretended that it is any longer the government of the U.S. — any government of Constitution and laws, — wherein a General, or a President, may make permanent rules of property by proclamation?

I do not say Congress might not with propriety pass a law, on the point, just such as General Fremont proclaimed. I do not say I might not, as a member of Congress, vote for it. What I object to, is, that I as President, shall expressly or impliedly seize and exercise the permanent legislative functions of the government.

So much as to principle. Now as to policy. No doubt the thing was popular in some quarters, and would have been more so if it had been a general declaration of emancipation. The Kentucky Legislature would

not budge till that proclamation was modified; and Gen. Anderson tele-
graphed me that on the news of Gen. Fremont having actually issued
deeds of manumission, a whole company of our Volunteers threw down
their arms and disbanded.[1] I was so assured, as to think it probable, that
the very arms we had furnished Kentucky would be turned against us.
I think to lose Kentucky is nearly the same as to lose the whole game.
Kentucky gone, we can not hold Missouri, nor, as I think, Maryland.
These all against us, and the job on our hands is too large for us. We
would as well consent to separation at once, including the surrender
of this capitol. On the contrary, if you will give up your restlessness for
new positions, and back me manfully on the grounds upon which you
and other kind friends gave me the election, and have approved in my
public documents, we shall go through triumphantly.

[1] *Manumission* is a legal term for emancipation, and a deed of manumission is a legal
document establishing the freedom of the holder. The Kentucky legislature had passed
a resolution demanding that Frémont's proclamation be revoked. The General Anderson
to whom Lincoln refers is Robert Anderson, the onetime commander of Fort Sumter,
who was now in command of the Department of Kentucky.

9

PACIFIC APPEAL

Editorial on Emancipation
June 14, 1862

*On May 9, 1862, Union general David Hunter, who oversaw the
occupying forces in South Carolina, Georgia, and Florida, issued a
proclamation announcing martial law in the region and declaring
slaves there immediately and "forever free." Lincoln revoked the order
by a proclamation explaining that only he, as commander in chief, had
the authority to emancipate slaves in rebellious areas and that he hoped
Union slave states would soon adopt his recommendations for gradual
emancipation. Lincoln's action drew a protest from the Pacific Appeal, a
black abolitionist newspaper founded in San Francisco in April 1862.*

From Editorial, *Pacific Appeal*, June 14, 1862.

We have refrained, hitherto, from commenting on President Lincoln's Pro-slavery Proclamation in reference to the proclamation issued by Gen. Hunter, declaring the slaves free in the department of the South, over which he had military command, in hopes that the President only denied that Gen. Hunter had "been authorized by the Government to make any proclamation declaring slaves free," in order that action in the premises might come from the highest source, *i.e.* the President himself, moreover he intimates in his proclamation that he is yet undecided. . . .

Recent dispatches, however, have given us to understand that the Cabinet has revoked Gen. Hunter's proclamation, and hence slavery is still recognized in the department of the South. We thought from President Lincoln's confiscation messages, his emancipation recommendations and other liberal actions, that it was his intention to strike at the root of the tree of strife. We supposed he was possessed of judgment sufficient to know that it was useless to lop off the extraneous branches, and leave the trunk of . . . discord and disunion—slavery—still standing to branch forth again and diffuse its malignant and pestiferous poison over the land; and we still hope he will abide by the principles he has hitherto avowed, on the strengths of which he was elected. . . .

We fear the Administration is pursuing a course detrimental to the best interests of the country, and encouraging the Rebels in their efforts to overthrow the Union, and perpetuate slavery.

Generals who are on the ground where slavery exists, and see what effects emancipation would produce, are the best judges when to strike the blow, and, by eradicating the evil, end the war.

We also fear, by the course he is pursuing, the President will alienate his ablest generals from him, and he will be unable to find capable men to take command of departments most infected with the evil.

10

GEORGE B. McCLELLAN

Harrison's Landing Letter

July 7, 1862

By July 1, 1862, Confederate general Robert E. Lee had successfully defended Richmond against the Peninsula Campaign of Union general George B. McClellan, who had marched his army northward between the James and York rivers. After stalling just miles from Richmond, McClellan withdrew his army to Harrison's Landing, on the James River. McClellan then penned a public letter to President Lincoln expressing his view of how to prosecute the war. Aware of calls by some in the Union to fight a fiercer war against civilian populations—Congress was debating the Second Confiscation Act as McClellan had approached Richmond— the general criticized any hardening of the Union war policy but conceded that wartime emancipation of some slaves, with compensation to loyal owners, might be necessary. McClellan's letter was especially popular with "War Democrats," members of the Democratic Party who never stopped believing that the Union could be restored by military action that did not include widespread emancipation. (Their opponents in the party, the "Peace Democrats," thought that even military force was unneces- sary. They hoped to negotiate a peace with the Confederacy.) Lincoln counted on the support of the War Democrats at the start of the war, but he alienated them as he moved toward emancipation. In 1864, the War Democrats secured the nomination of McClellan as the Democratic can- didate for president, and they circulated this letter widely as a campaign document.

This rebellion has assumed the character of a war. As such it should be regarded, and it should be conducted upon the highest principles known to Christian civilization. It should not be a war looking to the subjugation of the people of any State in any event. It should not be at all a war upon population, but against armed forces and political organiza- tions. Neither confiscation of property, political executions of persons,

From *War of the Rebellion: The Official Records of the Union and Confederate Armies* (Washington, D.C.: Government Printing Office, 1884), ser. 1, 11, pt. 1:73–74.

territorial organization of States, or forcible abolition of slavery should be contemplated for a moment.

In prosecuting the war all private property and unarmed persons should be strictly protected, subject only to the necessity of military operations; all private property taken for military use should be paid or receipted for; pillage and waste should be treated as high crimes, all unnecessary trespass sternly prohibited, and offensive demeanor by the military toward citizens promptly rebuked. Military arrests should not be tolerated, except in places where active hostilities exist, and oaths not required by enactments constitutionally made should be neither demanded nor received. Military government should be confined to the preservation of public order and the protection of political rights. Military power should not be allowed to interfere with the relations of servitude, either by supporting or impairing the authority of the master, except for repressing disorder, as in other cases. Slaves, contraband under the act of Congress, seeking military protection, should receive it. The right of the Government to appropriate permanently to its own service claims to slave labor should be asserted, and the right of the owner to compensation therefore should be recognized. This principle might be extended, upon grounds of military necessity and security, to all the slaves of a particular State, thus working manumission in such State; and in Missouri, perhaps in Western Virginia also, and possibly even in Maryland, the expediency of such a measure is only a question of time. A system of policy thus constitutional, and pervaded by the influences of Christianity and freedom, would receive the support of almost all truly loyal men, would deeply impress the rebel masses and all foreign nations, and it might be humbly hoped that it would commend itself to the favor of the Almighty.

Unless the principles governing the future conduct of our struggle shall be made known and approved the effort to obtain requisite forces will be almost hopeless. A declaration of radical views, especially upon slavery, will rapidly disintegrate our present armies.

11

SAMUEL J. KIRKWOOD

Letter to Henry W. Halleck

August 5, 1862

The Second Confiscation Act, signed into law by Lincoln on July 17, 1862, broadened the scope of emancipation. Whereas the First Confiscation Act the year before confiscated and liberated only those slaves put to labor by Confederates, the second act declared "forever free" all slaves who were owned by rebels and who were captured by Union forces or came into Union lines. The act left the fate of the freed people vague. While Lincoln continued to support efforts to colonize freed people abroad, many demanded that ex-slaves and other African Americans be allowed to fight for the Union. At the same time that it passed the Second Confiscation Act, Congress passed the Militia Act, which authorized military authorities to hire blacks, declare them emancipated, and emancipate their wives and children—if their owners supported the rebellion. However, the most common view among leading Union officials in mid-1862 was that African Americans were not suitable for combat. Governor Samuel J. Kirkwood of Iowa explained to General in Chief Henry W. Halleck why he supported blacks in the military so long as they were used for manual labor only.

You will bear me witness I have [no] trouble on the "*negro*" subject but there is as it seems to me so much good sense in the following extract from a letter to me from one of the best colonels this state has in the service.... It is as follows. "I hope under the confiscation and emancipation bill just passed by Congress to supply my regiment with a sufficient number of 'contrabands' to do all the 'extra duty' labor of my camp. I have now *sixty men on extra duty* as teamsters &c. whose places could just as well be filled with *niggers*. We do not need a single negro in the army to fight but we could use to good advantage about one hundred & fifty with a regiment as teamsters & for making roads, chopping wood[,]

From Samuel J. Kirkwood to Henry W. Halleck, August 5, 1862, RG 108, ser. 22, Letters Received by the Headquarters of the Army, 1827–1903, file K-493 (1862), National Archives, Washington, D.C.

policing camp &c. *There are enough soldiers on extra duty in the army to take Richmond or any other rebel city if they were in the ranks instead of doing negro work.*"

I have but one remark to add and that in regard to the negroes fighting—it is this—When the war is over & we have summed up the entire loss of life it has imposed on the country I shall not have any regrets if it is found that a part of the dead are *niggers* and that *all* are not white men.

3

Making the Emancipation Proclamation

In the first year of the war, Lincoln kept his campaign promise not to outlaw slavery where it already existed, although he encouraged gradual, compensated emancipation in the Border States and signed acts allowing the military to confiscate and emancipate slaves of rebellious owners in the Confederacy. Even as Congress took aim at slavery where it could—not only by supporting the contraband policy but also by prohibiting slavery in Washington, D.C., and the federal territories—Lincoln continued to take a moderate approach to emancipation through the spring of 1862, arguing that a more aggressive policy would alienate Border State Unionists and War Democrats whose support he saw as essential to the Union war effort. Pressure from antislavery activists (Documents 12 and 13), coupled with the lack of military success, led Lincoln to begin considering some sort of emancipation proclamation, which he would justify as an act of military necessity.

By mid-July 1862, the president was ready to act. On July 13, while on a carriage ride with Secretary of State William H. Seward and Secretary of War Edwin M. Stanton, Lincoln remarked that he was considering a proclamation to free the slaves. On July 17, he signed the Second Confiscation Act, which empowered him as commander in chief to implement emancipation measures against rebellious slaveowners. On July 22, he presented a draft of the Emancipation Proclamation to his cabinet, which advised him not to issue the Proclamation until after a Union military victory. Otherwise, it might appear as the desperate measure of a nearly defeated country. Lincoln agreed to wait. While he waited, he received criticism from abolitionists for not doing enough against slavery (Document 14), as well as rebukes from conservative northerners for not doing more to reverse the antislavery actions of Congress and the military. A Union success finally came on September 17 at the Battle of Antietam (or Sharpsburg) in western Maryland. Although the battle ended more in a stalemate than in a clear Union victory—General George B. McClellan repelled General Robert E. Lee's invading forces from Maryland without securing their surrender—Lincoln issued the preliminary Proclamation (Document 15). The preliminary Proclamation of September 22 gave rebels one hundred days to disband. If the rebellion continued on January 1, 1863, Lincoln would issue the final Emancipation Proclamation, which would declare free all slaves in areas in rebellion.

Reaction to the Proclamation was mixed. Predictably, Republican newspapers favored the measure while Democratic organs were against it. Benjamin R. Curtis, a former U.S. Supreme Court Justice, denounced the measure as unconstitutional (Document 16). Pro-Lincoln attorneys like Grosvenor P. Lowrey came to Lincoln's defense and declared the Proclamation a perfectly legal use of the president's war power (Document 17). Artists who already admired Lincoln now integrated icons of emancipation into their portraits of him (Document 18). Those who despised the president added the Proclamation to the set of symbols they drew on in their graphic condemnations of him (Document 19). Lincoln defended the Proclamation in his Annual Message to Congress in December but suggested that it allowed for slavery to be ended gradually in those areas unaffected by the measure (Document 20). African Americans and their white abolitionist allies were dismayed by Lincoln's suggestion in the message that slavery might survive in the country until as late as 1900 (Document 25).

The Confederacy fought as fiercely as ever after the preliminary Proclamation—Lee's army delivered a humiliating defeat to Union forces at Fredericksburg in mid-December—so Lincoln delivered on his threat. On January 1, 1863, he signed the final Emancipation Proclamation, which declared "forever free" all slaves in rebellious areas (Document 21). The Proclamation did not mention the Border States, as they had never joined the rebellion, and it exempted a number of areas—including southern Louisiana, eastern Tennessee, and western Virginia—occupied by Union armies or demonstrating strong Unionist sentiment (the western Virginia counties would soon become the new state of West Virginia, which prohibited slavery). More than any other wartime act, the Proclamation made the Civil War a war of emancipation. Conservatives battered Lincoln with criticism (Documents 23 and 24). Abolitionists applauded the Proclamation (Documents 22 and 26) but objected to the exemptions and demanded that Lincoln do more to establish legal equality for African Americans, despite the fact that the final Proclamation dropped colonization schemes in favor of the enlistment of blacks into the Union military.

12

LYDIA MARIA CHILD

Letter to John Greenleaf Whittier
January 21, 1862

A prolific author and antislavery leader, Lydia Maria Child was a Massachusetts abolitionist who had called for universal emancipation and black enlistment in the military from the start of the war. Child had followed closely the activities of Colonel James Montgomery, who was an early supporter of the recruitment of African Americans into the Union army. Montgomery had fought for Kansas as a free state in the 1850s, making an alliance there with John Brown. When the Civil War broke out, Montgomery became a colonel in James H. Lane's brigade of Kansans, who on their own authority created one of the earliest black regiments. Like Child, John Greenleaf Whittier, an accomplished poet, was a Massachusetts abolitionist who pressured the Lincoln administration for more decisive action against slavery. In early 1862, Child and Whittier, along with Harriet Tubman, the most famous operator on the antebellum Underground Railroad, recruited teachers, missionaries, and others committed to smoothing the transition from slavery to freedom, sending them to Union-occupied areas of the South Carolina and Georgia low country to assist the freed people there (see Document 32). Child and Whittier did not make the trip themselves, but Tubman did, as did Colonel Montgomery, who in South Carolina in 1863 organized an African American brigade, which included the Fifty-fourth Massachusetts Volunteer Infantry under the command of Robert Gould Shaw.

I fear greatly that there is not virtue enough left in the country to make salvation possible. Slavery seems to have poisoned the fountains of our national life. I do not know whether it is in the Providence of God to allow us to be an *example* to the nations, or whether He intends to use us as a *warning*. If we are saved, it will be better than we *deserve*. I would sacrifice everything in life, and life itself, to preserve our fine institutions,

---

From Lydia Maria Child to John Greenleaf Whittier, January 21, 1862, Lydia Maria Child Papers, Manuscript Division, Library of Congress, Washington, D.C.

but if we *must* have the noble structure pulled down . . . by the blind giant Slavery, I hope the poor negroes will have a rollicking good time over its ruins. You have doubtless heard of Harriet Tubman, whom they call Moses, on account of the multitude she has brought out of bondage by her courage and ingenuity. She talks politics sometimes, and her uncouth utterance is wiser than the plans of politicians. She said, the other day: ". . . God's ahead of massa Linkum. God won't let massa Linkum beat de South till he do *de right-ting*. Massa Linkum he great man, and I'se poor nigger; but dis nigger can tell massa Linkum how to save de money and de young men. He do it by setting de niggers free. . . ."[1]

. . . This winter I have, for the first time, been knitting for the army; but I do it only for *Kansas* troops. I can trust *them*; for they have vowed a vow unto the Lord that no fugitive shall ever be surrendered in *their* camps. There is a nephew of Kossuth[2] within Col. Montgomery's regiment. A few weeks ago, when he was on scout duty, a mulatto woman implored him to take her to the Yankee camp where her husband was. The mistress rushed out in hot pursuit. The young Hungarian reined in his horse, and called out to the slave, "Jump up, and hold on by me." She sprung on the horse, and they galloped away, under a shower of wrathful words from the mistress. When they rode into the Kansas camp all the soldiers threw up their caps and harraed, and Col. Montgomery called out "Three cheers for the Union!" This Col. Montgomery is a brave, God-fearing man, of the Puritan stamp, very much like his friend old John Brown.

---

[1] The story of Tubman's critique of Lincoln circulated widely, though no one knows exactly what she said. Tubman was quite articulate, but tellers of the story, including Child, often had her speak in the dialect of a poorly educated African American. Like other authors of the era, Child used such dialect to suggest an authentic African American voice, but many African Americans would have found the language insulting.

[2] Lajos Kossuth was a famous Hungarian reformer who helped establish a liberal democracy in his country in the 1840s and then, in 1851, went on a well-publicized tour of Great Britain and the United States.

13

FREDERICK DOUGLASS

The Slaveholders' Rebellion

July 4, 1862

Douglass delivered a stinging criticism of Lincoln in the speech "The Slaveholders' Rebellion," in Himrods Corners, New York, close to Rochester. Little did the abolitionist know that Lincoln was already contemplating an emancipation proclamation such as Douglass recommended or that Lincoln would sign into law a powerful emancipation measure, the Second Confiscation Act, only two weeks after the speech.

I come now to the policy of President Lincoln in reference to slavery. . . .
. . . Now what has been the tendency of his acts since he became Commander in Chief of the army and navy? I do not hesitate to say, that whatever may have been his intentions, the action of President Lincoln has been calculated in a marked and decided way to shield and protect slavery from the very blows which its horrible crimes have loudly and persistently invited. He has scornfully rejected the policy of arming the slaves, a policy naturally suggested and enforced by the nature and necessities of the war. He has steadily refused to proclaim, as he had the constitutional and moral right to proclaim, complete emancipation to all the slaves of rebels who should make their way into the lines of our army. He has repeatedly interfered with, and arrested the anti-slavery policy of some of his most earnest and reliable generals. He has assigned to the most important positions, generals who are notoriously pro-slavery, and hostile to the party and principles which raised him to power. He has permitted rebels to recapture their runaway slaves in sight of the capital. He has allowed General Halleck, to openly violate the spirit of the solemn resolution of Congress forbidding the army of the United States to return the fugitive slaves to their cruel

---

From Frederick Douglass, "The Slaveholders' Rebellion," *Douglass' Monthly*, August 1862, 692–93.

masters,[3] and has evidently from the first submitted himself to the guidance of the half loyal slave States, rather than the wise and loyal suggestions of those States upon which must fall, and have fallen, the chief expense and danger involved in the prosecution of the war. It is from such action as this that we must infer the policy of the Administration. To my mind that policy is simply and solely to reconstruct the union on the cold and corrupting basis of compromise; by which slavery shall retain all the power that it has ever had, with the full assurance of gaining more, according to its future necessities.

The question now arises, "Is such a reconstruction possible or desirable?" To this I answer from the depths of my soul, no. Mr. Lincoln is powerful, Mr. Lincoln can do many things, but Mr. Lincoln will never see the day when he can bring back or charm back, the scattered fragments of the Union into the shape and form they stood when they were shattered by this slaveholding rebellion.

. . . You must abolish slavery or abandon the union. It is plain that there can never be any union between the north and the south, while the south values slavery more than nationality. A union of interest is essential to a union of ideas, and without this union of ideas, the outward form of the union will be but a rope of sand. . . . But it is asked how will you abolish slavery. You have no power over the system before the rebellion is suppressed, and you will have no right or power when it is suppressed. I will answer this argument when I have stated how the thing will be done. The fact is there will be no trouble about the way, if only the government possessed the will. But several ways have been suggested. One is a stringent Confiscation Bill by Congress. Another is by a proclamation by the President at the head of the nation. Another is by the commanders of each division of the army. There is plausibility in the argument that we cannot reach slavery until we have suppressed the rebellion. Yet it is far more true to say that we cannot reach the rebellion until we have suppressed slavery. For slavery is the life of the rebellion. Let the loyal army but inscribe upon its banner, Emancipation and protection to all those who will rally under it, and no power could prevent a stampede from slavery, such as the world has not witnessed since the Hebrews crossed the Red Sea. I am convinced that this rebellion and

---

[3] On March 13, 1862, Congress passed a resolution forbidding the return of slaves who escaped to Union lines. General Henry W. Halleck, the highest-ranking officer in the West and soon to become general in chief of the Union army, nevertheless ordered those under his command to turn away all slaves seeking refuge in Union lines. He defended his order by arguing that slaves allowed into Union lines might later return to their masters and betray valuable strategic information.

slavery are twin monsters, and that they must fall or flourish together, and that all attempts at upholding one while putting down the other will be followed by continued trains of darkening calamities, such as make this anniversary of our national independence a day of mourning instead of a day of transcendent joy and gladness.

But a proclamation of Emancipation, says one, would only be a paper order. . . . All Laws all written rules for the Government of the army and navy and people, are "paper orders," and would remain only such were they not backed up by force, still we do not object to them as useless, but admit their wisdom and necessity. Then these paper orders carry with them a certain moral force which makes them in a large measure self-executing. I know of none which would possess this self-executing power in larger measure than a proclamation of Emancipation.

14

ABRAHAM LINCOLN

Letter to Horace Greeley

August 22, 1862

Horace Greeley, the antislavery editor of the New York Tribune, *was the most famous newspaper editor of the Civil War era. On August 20, 1862, the* Tribune *published Greeley's "The Prayer of Twenty Millions," which criticized Lincoln for protecting slavery in the Border States and failing to give full support to military commanders who supported emancipation. The twenty million residents of the Union states, Greeley wrote, were "sorely disappointed and deeply pained by the policy you seem to be pursuing with regard to the slaves of Rebels."[4] Lincoln answered Greeley in a letter printed by the* Tribune *and reprinted throughout the Union and the Confederacy. Although Lincoln already had written the Emancipation Proclamation, he did not mention the document, choosing to stick to his strategy of waiting for a Union victory to issue it.*

[4] Horace Greeley, "The Prayer of Twenty Millions," *New York Tribune*, August 20, 1862.

From Roy P. Basler, ed., and Marion Dolores Pratt and Lloyd A. Dunlap, asst. eds., *The Collected Works of Abraham Lincoln* (New Brunswick, N.J.: Rutgers University Press, 1953–1955), 5:388–89.

As to the policy I "seem to be pursuing" as you say, I have not meant to leave any one in doubt.

I would save the Union. I would save it the shortest way under the Constitution. The sooner the national authority can be restored; the nearer the Union will be "the Union as it was." If there be those who would not save the Union, unless they could at the same time *save* slavery, I do not agree with them. If there be those who would not save the Union unless they could at the same time *destroy* slavery, I do not agree with them. My paramount object in this struggle *is* to save the Union, and is *not* either to save or to destroy slavery. If I could save the Union without freeing *any* slave I would do it, and if I could save it by freeing *all* the slaves I would do it; and if I could save it by freeing some and leaving others alone I would also do that. What I do about slavery, and the colored race, I do because I believe it helps to save the Union; and what I forbear, I forbear because I do *not* believe it would help to save the Union. I shall do *less* whenever I shall believe what I am doing hurts the cause, and I shall do *more* whenever I shall believe doing more will help the cause. I shall try to correct errors when shown to be errors; and I shall adopt new views so fast as they shall appear to be true views.

I have here stated my purpose according to my view of *official* duty; and I intend no modification of my oft-expressed *personal* wish that all men every where could be free.

15

ABRAHAM LINCOLN

Preliminary Emancipation Proclamation

September 22, 1862

When announcing his plan to emancipate all slaves in rebellious areas, Lincoln framed his order in terms of his dual role as commander in chief acting out of military necessity and chief executive fulfilling the mandates of Congress—specifically the act of March 13, 1862, prohibiting the

From Roy P. Basler, ed., and Marion Dolores Pratt and Lloyd A. Dunlap, asst. eds., *The Collected Works of Abraham Lincoln* (New Brunswick, N.J.: Rutgers University Press, 1953–1955), 5:433–36.

return of slaves coming into Union lines, and the Second Confiscation Act of July 17, 1862. One of the controversial clauses of the preliminary Proclamation was the order to the armed forces not to repress the actions that slaves "may make for their actual freedom." In effect, this passage simply echoed the congressional act prohibiting the military from turning back fugitive slaves, but many read Lincoln — wrongly — as attempting to incite slave insurrections.

I, Abraham Lincoln, President of the United States of America, and Commander-in-chief of the Army and Navy thereof, do hereby proclaim and declare that hereafter, as heretofore, the war will be prossecuted for the object of practically restoring the constitutional relation between the United States, and each of the states, and the people thereof, in which states that relation is, or may be suspended, or disturbed.

That it is my purpose, upon the next meeting of Congress to again recommend the adoption of a practical measure tendering pecuniary aid to the free acceptance or rejection of all slave-states, so called, the people whereof may not then be in rebellion against the United States, and which states, may then have voluntarily adopted, or thereafter may voluntarily adopt, immediate, or gradual abolishment of slavery within their respective limits; and that the effort to colonize persons of African descent, with their consent, upon this continent, or elsewhere, with the previously obtained consent of the Governments existing there, will be continued.[5]

That on the first day of January in the year of our Lord, one thousand eight hundred and sixty-three, all persons held as slaves within any state, or designated part of a state, the people whereof shall then be in rebellion against the United States shall be then, thenceforward, and forever free; and the executive government of the United States, including the military and naval authority thereof, will recognize and maintain the freedom of such persons, and will do no act or acts to repress such persons, or any of them, in any efforts they may make for their actual freedom.

That the executive will, on the first day of January aforesaid, by proclamation, designate the States, and parts of states, if any, in which the people thereof respectively, shall then be in rebellion against the United

---

[5] Lincoln had already approved a plan for the colonization of African Americans in Chiriquí, in present-day Panama, but he had abandoned the plan when governments in the region protested that it violated treaties protecting their sovereignty.

States; and the fact that any state, or the people thereof shall, on that day be, in good faith represented in the Congress of the United States, by members chosen thereto, at elections wherein a majority of the qualified voters of such state shall have participated, shall, in the absence of strong countervailing testimony, be deemed conclusive evidence that such state and the people thereof, are not then in rebellion against the United States.

That attention is hereby called to an act of Congress entitled "An act to make an additional Article of War" approved March 13, 1862. . . .

Also to the ninth and tenth sections of an act entitled "An Act to suppress Insurrection, to punish Treason and Rebellion, to seize and confiscate property of rebels, and for other purposes," approved July 17, 1862. . . .

And I do hereby enjoin upon and order all persons engaged in the military and naval service of the United States to observe, obey, and enforce, within their respective spheres of service, the act, and sections above recited.

And the executive will in due time recommend that all citizens of the United States who shall have remained loyal thereto throughout the rebellion, shall (upon the restoration of the constitutional relation between the United States, and their respective states, and people, if that relation shall have been suspended or disturbed) be compensated for all losses by acts of the United States, including the loss of slaves.

16

BENJAMIN R. CURTIS

Executive Power

1862

Massachusetts attorney Benjamin R. Curtis graduated from Harvard Law School and served on the U.S. Supreme Court from 1851 to 1857. In 1857, he dissented from the majority opinion in the Dred Scott *case, arguing that Congress did have the power to prohibit slavery in the*

From B. R. Curtis, *Executive Power* (Cambridge, Mass.: H. O. Houghton, 1862), 21, 25.

territories and that Scott should be a free man. His discontent led him to retire from the Court and return to private practice in Massachusetts. Believing that Lincoln had overreached his military authority in issuing the Emancipation Proclamation, he published the pamphlet Executive Power, *contending that legislative power was supreme, an argument he had made in his* Dred Scott *dissent. In particular, Curtis upheld the power of states to make their own laws regarding slavery and denied the authority of the president to violate those laws, even in times of war.*

All the powers of the President are executive merely. He cannot make a law. He cannot repeal one. He can only execute laws. He can neither make, nor suspend, nor alter them. He cannot even make an article of war. He may govern the army, either by general or special orders, but only in subordination to the Constitution and laws of the United States, and the articles of war enacted by the legislative power. . . .

What then, is [the commander in chief's] authority over the persons and property of citizens? I answer that, over all persons enlisted in his forces he has military power and command; that over all persons and property *within the sphere of his actual operations in the field*, he may lawfully exercise such restraint and control as the successful prosecution of his particular military enterprise may, in his honest judgment, absolutely require; and upon such persons as have committed offences against any article of war, he may, through appropriate military tribunals, inflict the punishment prescribed by law. *And there his lawful authority ends.*

The military power over citizens and their property is a power to *act*, not a power to prescribe rules for *future* action. It springs from present pressing emergencies, and is limited by them. It cannot assume the functions of the statesman or legislator, and make provision for future or distant arrangements by which persons or property may be made subservient to military uses. . . .

But when the military commander controls the persons or property of citizens, who are beyond the sphere of his actual operations in the field when he makes laws to govern their conduct, he becomes a legislator. Those laws may be made actually operative; obedience to them may be enforced by military power; their purpose and effect may be solely to recruit or support his armies, or to weaken the power of the enemy with which he is contending. *But he is legislator still*; and whether his edicts are clothed in the form of proclamations, or military orders, or by whatever name they may be called, they are laws.

17

GROSVENOR P. LOWREY

The Commander-in-Chief

1862

Grosvenor P. Lowrey was a well-known New York attorney who, at the urging of Lincoln supporters, published a legal defense of the Emancipation Proclamation in response to Benjamin Curtis's pamphlet (Document 16). Lowrey's pamphlet was published in late 1862 and then reprinted in 1863, after Lincoln signed the final Emancipation Proclamation.

The duties of the Commander-in-chief are divisible into two classes: those routine duties, fixed by law under the authority of Congress to "raise and support armies," such as organization of the army, appointment of officers, &c., which belong equally to peace and war; and those other undefined duties which arise only in time of war. . . . The fundamental fallacy of Judge Curtis' pamphlet is, that he utterly confounds these two classes of powers, as well as the difference between the rules applicable in war to the citizen, and those applicable to the enemy. . . .

What is that which *he* [the Commander-in-chief] proposes? To set free, by force of military power, and as a measure of offence and defence, the slaves of rebellious communities. In other words, there are in the rebellious communities, which it is the duty of the Commander-in-chief to subdue, a great number of persons actively engaged in supporting the war, by providing subsistence for the rebel armies. They are forcibly held to this service by the same men, and the same inimical authority, which are now assaulting the life of the nation. In the interest of the nation, and for the purpose of weakening the enemy, the Commander-in-chief proposes to disregard and invite the persons so held, to disregard this local authority, and cease to serve it. . . .

From Grosvenor P. Lowrey, *The Commander-in-Chief; Defence upon Legal Grounds of the Proclamation of Emancipation; and an Answer to Ex-Judge Curtis' Pamphlet, Entitled "Executive Power,"* 2nd ed. (New York: G. P. Putnam, 1863), 14, 20–21.

[The Emancipation Proclamation] "repeals and annuls valid state laws," says [Judge Curtis]. Were this the effect, or the attempt, it would be startling; for the spectacle of a civil system, overturned, destroyed, repealed, or annulled, by arbitrary military force, is not an inviting one for the eyes of constitutional republicans, even where the system is that of an enemy.

But such is neither the intent nor possible consequence. The act being military, is capable to produce only a military result. The military power suspends, but never destroys the law. So well has its effect been understood for ages, that it has grown into a maxim: *Inter arma silent leges.*[6] But though military power never destroys the law, its very first and principal effect is to destroy rights and things existing under the law. It is this which constitutes war. It may also suspend the relation between persons and things, under such circumstances, that the right or relation can never be restored.

[6] "In the midst of war, the law is silent."

18

EDWARD DALTON MARCHANT

Abraham Lincoln

1863

Two months after Lincoln issued the preliminary Emancipation Procla-mation, the Philadelphia artist Edward Marchant received a commission from the Union Club of Philadelphia to paint a dramatization of the president writing the document. Lincoln agreed to pose for Marchant, and the final painting, which the artist completed in 1863, was widely copied and distributed in 1864. On Lincoln's desk is the Emancipation Proclamation. Above his left shoulder is a broken chain dangling around the foot of a statue of a female slave.

Edward Dalton Marchant, *Abraham Lincoln, Sixteenth President of the United States,* engraved by John Sartrain (Philadelphia: Bradley & Co., 1864).

19

ADALBERT JOHANN VOLCK

Writing the Emancipation Proclamation

1863

Adalbert Volck was a Confederate sympathizer who was born in Prussia and lived in Baltimore. A dentist by training, Volck etched as a hobby. During the Civil War, he drew and privately circulated a number of anti-Union images. In this drawing, as Lincoln drafts the Emancipation Proclamation, he rests his foot on the Constitution and draws ink from a well embraced by the devil. Two images hanging behind Lincoln

Adalbert Johann Volck, *Writing the Emancipation Proclamation, Confederate War Etchings*, no. 3 (privately published, n.d.).

suggest his radical tendencies. The first depicts John Brown as a saint. The second shows the St. Domingue slave revolt. A bottle of liquor figures prominently in one corner, suggesting that Lincoln was drunk when he wrote the Proclamation. (In fact, Lincoln had always abstained from alcohol.) In the other corner, a Scottish cap covers the head of the statue of Lady Columbia, the symbol of the Republic. The cap was a common icon of anti-Lincoln imagery: It played on the rumor that Lincoln had sneaked cowardly into Washington to take office in 1861 wearing a "Scotch cap" to disguise himself so that he would not be attacked. To Lincoln's right, a vulture's head holds back the curtain, revealing vultures outside ready to feed on a country ruined by the Proclamation.

20

ABRAHAM LINCOLN

Annual Message to Congress

December 1, 1862

In his preliminary Emancipation Proclamation, Lincoln announced that he would deliver further information about his efforts on behalf of gradual, compensated emancipation, with colonization, at the next meeting of Congress. His annual message to Congress — which, as was customary, was read to Congress by a clerk — contained the information promised in the form of three proposed constitutional amendments. The first two amendments offered compensation to former masters who had remained loyal to the Union. The third authorized colonization of African Americans. Lincoln had abandoned a colonization plan for the Central American state of Chiriquí in favor of one for Île à Vache, a small island off the southwest coast of Haiti. Because the island was privately owned

From Roy P. Basler, ed., and Marion Dolores Pratt and Lloyd A. Dunlap, asst. eds., *The Collected Works of Abraham Lincoln* (New Brunswick, N.J.: Rutgers University Press, 1953–1955), 5:529–31, 536–37.

and outside any nation's sovereignty, the plan avoided the treaty problems that had thwarted the Chiriquí scheme. Although Lincoln's proposed amendments reaffirmed the commitment to emancipation he had made in the preliminary Emancipation Proclamation, they might have allowed slavery to survive in some areas of the nation until 1900.

I recommend the adoption of the following resolution and articles amendatory to the Constitution of the United States. . . .

"Article —.

"Every State, wherein slavery now exists, which shall abolish the same therein, at any time, or times, before the first day of January, in the year of our Lord one thousand and nine hundred, shall receive compensation from the United States. . . .

"Article —.

"All slaves who shall have enjoyed actual freedom by the chances of the war, at any time before the end of the rebellion, shall be forever free; but all owners of such, who shall not have been disloyal, shall be compensated for them, at the same rates as is provided for States adopting abolishment of slavery, but in such way, that no slave shall be twice accounted for.

"Article —.

"Congress may appropriate money, and otherwise provide, for colonizing free colored persons, with their own consent, at any place or places without the United States."

I beg indulgence to discuss these proposed articles at some length. Without slavery the rebellion could never have existed; without slavery it could not continue.

Among the friends of the Union there is great diversity, of sentiment, and of policy, in regard to slavery, and the African race amongst us. Some would perpetuate slavery; some would abolish it suddenly, and without compensation; some would abolish it gradually, and with compensation; some would remove the freed people from us, and some would retain them with us; and there are yet other minor diversities. Because of these diversities, we waste much strength in struggles among ourselves. By mutual concession we should harmonize, and act together. This would be compromise; but it would be compromise among the friends, and not with the enemies of the Union. These articles are intended to embody a plan of such mutual concessions. If the plan shall be adopted, it is assumed that emancipation will follow, at least, in several of the States. . . .

This plan is recommended as a means, not in exclusion of, but additional to, all others for restoring and preserving the national authority throughout the Union. The subject is presented exclusively in its economical aspect. The plan would, I am confident, secure peace more speedily, and maintain it more permanently, than can be done by force alone; while all it would cost, considering amounts, and manner of payment, and times of payment, would be easier paid than will be the additional cost of the war, if we rely solely upon force. . . . It would cost no blood at all.

The plan is proposed as permanent constitutional law. It cannot become such without the concurrence of, first, two-thirds of Congress, and, afterwards, three-fourths of the States. The requisite three-fourths of the States will necessarily include seven of the Slave states. Their concurrence, if obtained, will give assurance of their severally adopting emancipation, at no very distant day, upon the new constitutional terms. This assurance would end the struggle now, and save the Union forever. . . .

Is it doubted, then, that the plan I propose, if adopted, would shorten the war, and thus lessen its expenditure of money and of blood? Is it doubted that it would restore the national authority and national prosperity, and perpetuate both indefinitely? Is it doubted that we here—Congress and Executive—can secure its adoption? Will not the good people respond to a united, and earnest appeal from us? Can we, can they, by any other means, so certainly, or so speedily, assure these vital objects? We can succeed only by concert. It is not "can *any* of us *imagine* better?" but "can we *all* do better?" Object whatsoever is possible, still the question recurs "can we do better?" The dogmas of the quiet past, are inadequate to the stormy present. The occasion is piled high with difficulty, and we must rise with the occasion. As our case is new, so we must think anew, and act anew. We must disenthrall our selves, and then we shall save our country.

Fellow-citizens, *we* cannot escape history. We of this Congress and this administration, will be remembered in spite of ourselves. No personal significance, or insignificance, can spare one or another of us. The fiery trial through which we pass, will light us down, in honor or dishonor, to the latest generation. We *say* we are for the Union. The world will not forget that we say this. We know how to save the Union. The world knows we do know how to save it. We—even *we here*—hold the power, and bear the responsibility. In *giving* freedom to the *slave*, we *assure* freedom to the *free*—honorable alike in what we give, and what we preserve. We shall nobly save, or meanly lose, the last best, hope of earth. Other means may succeed; this could not fail. The way is plain, peaceful, generous, just—a way which, if followed, the world will forever applaud, and God must forever bless.

21

ABRAHAM LINCOLN

Final Emancipation Proclamation

January 1, 1863

As promised in his preliminary Proclamation, Lincoln issued his final Emancipation Proclamation on January 1, 1863. Unlike the preliminary Proclamation, the final version specified the areas to be affected. Exempted were the Border States; some areas in the Confederacy where there was strong Unionist support, such as eastern Tennessee; and most areas under Union army occupation, including southern Louisiana. Also exempted were the western counties of Virginia, which became the free state of West Virginia.

By the President of the United States of America:

A Proclamation.

Whereas, on the twentysecond day of September, in the year of our Lord one thousand eight hundred and sixty two, a proclamation was issued by the President of the United States, containing, among other things, the following, towit:

"That on the first day of January, in the year of our Lord one thousand eight hundred and sixty-three, all persons held as slaves within any State or designated part of a State, the people whereof shall then be in rebellion against the United States, shall be then, thenceforward, and forever free; and the Executive Government of the United States, including the military and naval authority thereof, will recognize and maintain the freedom of such persons, and will do no act or acts to repress such

From Roy P. Basler, ed., and Marion Dolores Pratt and Lloyd A. Dunlap, asst. eds., *The Collected Works of Abraham Lincoln* (New Brunswick, N.J.: Rutgers University Press, 1953–1955), 6:28–30.

persons, or any of them, in any efforts they may make for their actual freedom.

"That the Executive will, on the first day of January aforesaid, by proclamation, designate the States and parts of States, if any, in which the people thereof, respectively, shall then be in rebellion against the United States; and the fact that any State, or the people thereof, shall on that day be, in good faith, represented in the Congress of the United States by members chosen thereto at elections wherein a majority of the qualified voters of such State shall have participated, shall, in the absence of strong countervailing testimony, be deemed conclusive evidence that such State, and the people thereof, are not then in rebellion against the United States."

Now, therefore I, Abraham Lincoln, President of the United States, by virtue of the power in me vested as Commander-in-Chief, of the Army and Navy of the United States in time of actual armed rebellion against authority and government of the United States, and as a fit and necessary war measure for suppressing said rebellion, do, on this first day of January, in the year of our Lord one thousand eight hundred and sixty three, and in accordance with my purpose so to do publicly proclaimed for the full period of one hundred days, from the day first above mentioned, order and designate as the States and parts of States wherein the people thereof respectively, are this day in rebellion against the United States, the following, towit:

Arkansas, Texas, Louisiana, (except the Parishes of St. Bernard, Plaquemines, Jefferson, St. Johns, St. Charles, St. James[,] Ascension, Assumption, Terrebonne, Lafourche, St. Mary, St. Martin, and Orleans, including the City of New-Orleans) Mississippi, Alabama, Florida, Georgia, South-Carolina, North-Carolina, and Virginia, (except the fortyeight counties designated as West Virginia, and also the counties of Berkley, Accomac, Northampton, Elizabeth-City, York, Princess Ann, and Norfolk, including the cities of Norfolk & Portsmouth [)]; and which excepted parts are, for the present, left precisely as if this proclamation were not issued.

And by virtue of the power, and for the purpose aforesaid, I do order and declare that all persons held as slaves within said designated States, and parts of States, are, and henceforward shall be free; and that the Executive government of the United States, including the military and naval authorities thereof, will recognize and maintain the freedom of said persons.

And I hereby enjoin upon the people so declared to be free to abstain from all violence, unless in necessary self-defence; and I recommend to them that, in all cases when allowed, they labor faithfully for reasonable wages.

And I further declare and make known, that such persons of suitable condition, will be received into the armed service of the United States to garrison forts, positions, stations, and other places, and to man vessels of all sorts in said service.

And upon this act, sincerely believed to be an act of justice, warranted by the Constitution, upon military necessity, I invoke the considerate judgment of mankind, and the gracious favor of Almighty God.

In witness whereof, I have hereunto set my hand and caused the seal of the United States to be affixed.

Done at the City of Washington, this first day of January, in the year of our Lord one thousand eight hundred and sixty three, and of the Independence of the United States of America the eighty-seventh.

By the President: ABRAHAM LINCOLN

22

PACIFIC APPEAL

The Year of Jubilee Has Come!

January 3, 1863

In the Judeo-Christian tradition, a jubilee was the periodic freeing of slaves (Lev. 25:10–13). Slaves and free African Americans had long spoken and sung of the "day of jubilee" to come, and many saw the signing of the Emancipation Proclamation as the fulfillment of that prophecy. Copies of the Proclamation circulated among slave communities (southern officials regularly punished, even executed, those found carrying copies), and African Americans already freed, including those in Union-occupied areas, held celebrations where the Proclamation was read. This brief editorial in the Pacific Appeal, *a black abolitionist paper in San Francisco, captured what the Proclamation signified to African Americans throughout the country.*

"The Year of Jubilee Has Come!" *Pacific Appeal*, January 3, 1863.

January 1, 1863

The anxiously looked-for day has arrived, . . . under the President's Proclamation, to untold numbers of slaves on American soil, who have writhed in agony under the galling chains of slavery, crying, with deep lamentations, "How long, how long, O Lord, before our deliverance shall come to pass?" To-day they are permitted, under the broad shield of the United States Government, to stand erect as men. To-day they arise above the status of mere bondsmen, allied to the brute creation of a property sense, by the soulless political theories of the impious slaveocracy. To-day the Government has washed its hands clean of the stains of slavery in the States and parts of the States that are in rebellion. America, henceforth, looms up with grandeur. She has burst the bands that have bound her, from her infancy to her maturity, and declares, before High Heaven, she must be free! Giant-like, she now appears, with her implements of war, not only to strike terror to traitors and domestic foes at home, but, with added strength from her loyal colored sons, she may with confidence hurl defiance at her enemies abroad. America, to-day, takes a proud stand, confronting the world with unabashed majesty.

23

CINCINNATI DAILY ENQUIRER

The Emancipation Proclamation
January 3, 1863

Most northern Democrats consistently opposed making emancipation a war aim. Union anti-emancipation sentiment was strongest in the lower Midwest, where the population, largely descended from white southerners, supported state "black laws," such as those of Ohio, Illinois, and Indiana. These laws denied African Americans certain civil rights, such as the right to testify in court. Democrats in these states, and in all the states throughout the Union, had denounced Lincoln's preliminary Emancipation Proclamation and had scored many victories in the fall elections of 1862 in part by running against the Proclamation. The Cincinnati

From "The Emancipation Proclamation," *Cincinnati Daily Enquirer,* January 3, 1863.

Enquirer was one of the most vocal and widely reprinted pro-Democratic, antiadministration papers.

We have thought that one great object Lincoln had in view in issuing this proclamation was to produce such a bitter hatred on the part of the South toward the North that, in the event the Southern Confederacy shall be acknowledged, it would never consent to any Northern State becoming a member of it. Sure it is that the South will shrink with horror and loathing from a connection with a people who would countenance the stirring up of servile insurrections among them, the inevitable concomitants of which are arson, rapine and the slaughter of women and children. The magnitude of the enormity is too great for the South ever to shake hands over with the North.

The proclamation will divide the North. There can be no unity of feeling, hereafter, at the North on the war. No true Democrat will support the war waged under that proclamation. It will be supported solely by Abolitionists. The line between the supporters and opposers of the war will, hereafter, be broad and unmistakable. The proclamation cuts off all Democratic sympathy with the object for which the war is to be prosecuted. The proclamation is thrown in the face, as if in derision, of the expression of Northern public sentiment at the recent elections. It is issued in contempt of the wishes of the people, who, in advance, expressed their disapprobation of it. It humiliates in the dust every Northern man, of noble heart, generous impulses and American pride. The idea that twenty millions of Northerners can not conquer eight millions of Southern men, without calling in the assistance of negroes, and using servile insurrection as an instrument, can not be other wise than humiliating to American pride.

It will paralyze the border slave States. Fear, not love, will keep them in their places; but though in place, they will not be in sympathy with the object for which the war is to be waged under the proclamation. They will know and feel that though they are not embraced by the proclamation, they might as well be; for what will their property be worth, with millions of liberated slaves on their borders. They can not but feel that hereafter the war is to be prosecuted, not to maintain the Union or to restore the Union, but for the destruction of slavery. It will be waged for conquest and subjugation, and to maintain the freedom of the millions of blacks declared free by this proclamation.

The radical Abolitionists now control the policy of the Administration. They have at last got the absolute control of Lincoln. They were determined the Union should never be restored with slavery. . . . But what a price they will have made the American people pay for it! The Abolition locomotive is now under full headway. We shall see where it will bring the country.

24

JAMES H. HUDSON

Letter to the Pacific Appeal

February 25, 1863

Despite the initial enthusiasm the Pacific Appeal *expressed for the Emancipation Proclamation, James H. Hudson, a correspondent for the newspaper writing from Suisun City, California, between San Francisco and Sacramento, offered a different opinion.*

I am one of those who think that the President has been too dilatory in seizing, for the use of the public, such potent means of oppressive warfare as a declaration of emancipation would have been 12 months ago, and even now, so far from perceiving the full requirements of the occasion — as, for instance, the necessity for complete and decisive measures for reducing the strength of the rebellion, — our honest but incompetent President adopts a half-way measure, which purports to give freedom to the bulk of the slave population beyond the reach of our arms, while it ignores or defies justice, by clinching the rivets of the chain which binds those whom alone we have present power to redeem. The proclamation should have been made to include every bondsman on the soil of America; every chain should have been broken, and the oppressed bidden to go free. Then, indeed, believing we were obeying the divine law, we might have invoked God's blessing upon our arms, and we could then have boldly claimed the services of every loyal man, white or black, in suppressing this hell-born and heaven-defying rebellion.

From James H. Hudson to *Pacific Appeal*, February 25, 1863, in *Pacific Appeal*, March 7, 1863.

25

HARPER'S WEEKLY

Sensation among "Our Colored Brethren"

December 20, 1862

The full caption of the cartoon, sketched by an unknown artist, was "Sensation among 'Our Colored Brethren,' on ascertaining that the Grand Performance to which they had been invited on New Year's Day, was unavoidably postponed to the year 1900!" Poised for liberation because of the promise of the preliminary Emancipation Proclamation of September 22, 1862, the slaves in the cartoon are dismayed to learn that Lincoln's message to Congress of December 1, 1862, recommended constitutional amendments that might allow slavery to exist until as late as 1900. "Our

"Sensation among 'Our Colored Brethren,'" *Harper's Weekly*, December 20, 1862, 816.

*Colored Brethren" was a longtime abolitionist phrase describing slaves
and free blacks. The sign in the store reads, "The Great Negro Emancipation Fandango Is Postponed Until 1900" and is signed "Abm. Lincoln,
Manager." The slave at the left carries a makeshift sack on which are
emblazoned the initials of Horace Greeley, the abolitionist editor who
pressured Lincoln to issue the Proclamation four months before. The
image criticizes Lincoln, who has betrayed the promise of the Proclamation, but it also mocks African Americans, who appear as dupes. The
artist uses common racist stereotypes of the era. The two central figures
of the image, the banjo player with his top hat and the raggedly clad field
hand, were familiar figures in northern minstrel shows of the nineteenth
century.*

26

THOMAS NAST

The Emancipation of the Negroes
January 24, 1863

*Thomas Nast, the best-known political sketch artist of the nineteenth cen-
tury, uses a montage of images to tell the story of slavery and emancipation. At the center is a black family at the moment of emancipation. A
portrait of Abraham Lincoln hangs above the fireplace. Beginning on the
upper left and moving counterclockwise, smaller scenes depict the experience of African Americans from the first days of the slave trade to their post-
emancipation experiences with wage labor (a black man collects money
from a cashier) and education (children head off to the public school).*

Thomas Nast, "The Emancipation of the Negroes, January, 1863—The Past and the
Future," *Harper's Weekly*, January 24, 1863, 56–57.

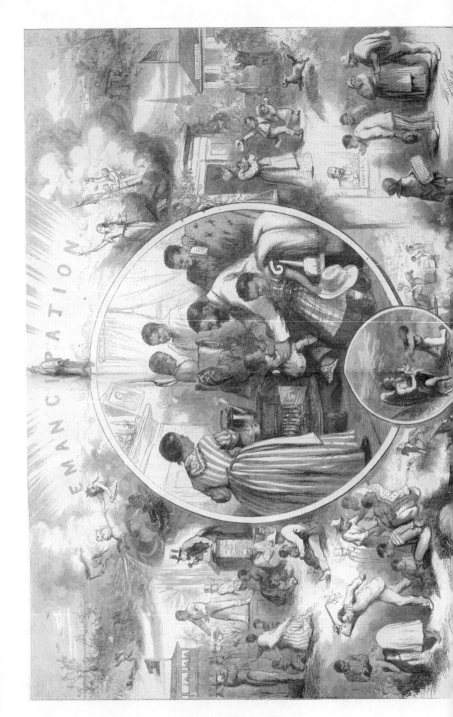

4

African Americans and Military Service

From the start of the Civil War, a number of slaves, free blacks, and white abolitionists urged Union authorities to allow African Americans to fight in the Union army and navy. The Union military allowed blacks into service, but only as manual laborers, not as soldiers. A few white commanders, most notably James H. Lane and James Montgomery in Kansas (see Document 12), recruited all-black regiments on their own, although the Union high command discouraged their actions. Meanwhile, a few African American volunteers were able to persuade enlisting officers or local officials to allow them to serve in all-white units (Document 27). In a November 1861 draft of his official report as U.S. secretary of war, Simon Cameron recommended enlisting blacks into the military. Lincoln rejected the proposal and eventually replaced Cameron with Edwin M. Stanton. As Lincoln prepared to issue the Emancipation Proclamation the following year, civilians and military officials pressed him to couple emancipation with black recruitment. Lincoln welcomed ex-slaves into the military as laborers in the final Proclamation and privately endorsed plans for creating African American regiments. After issuing the Proclamation, he never again publicly endorsed colonization for ex-slaves. He knew that blacks could serve the Union better as soldiers than as colonists abroad.

Early in 1863, the War Department created the Bureau of Colored Troops, which oversaw the creation of state and national regiments composed exclusively of African Americans. However, the War Department appointed only white commanders to black regiments and paid black soldiers only ten dollars a month, hardly enough to support a family and three dollars less than the monthly pay of white soldiers. The difference in pay galled African Americans (Document 33). As slaves, they had been counted as three-fifths of a person for purposes of representation in the House of Representatives. Now, as free people, they were making three-quarters of a white person's wage. Yet 70 percent of African American men of fighting age joined Union forces—a rate roughly three times that of qualified whites. When, in 1863, the Union government imposed a draft requiring states to supply specified numbers of soldiers, it allowed them to fill their quotas with black as well as white men. This policy helped build support among whites previously opposed to black enlistment. Whereas many whites backed black enlistment for purely pragmatic reasons, African Americans saw a higher purpose in the policy: They hoped or even assumed that it would lead to legal equality and full citizenship in the nation (Documents 28 and 29). Antislavery activists overseeing reconstruction programs in the South were inspired by the arrival of African Americans in Union uniforms (Document 32).

African Americans in Union uniform faced greater dangers than their white counterparts. They were more likely to be mistreated, even killed, if they were captured by Confederates (Document 30). Meanwhile, soldiers' wives and children who were still enslaved were likely to receive harsher treatment than ever before, as masters took out their frustration at losing slaves by heaping new abuses on those left behind (Document 31). African American soldiers advocated for new laws freeing their relatives, even if they lived in Union slave states, and they looked forward to the moment when they would march onto their former masters' land and liberate their families by force (Document 34).

27

H. FORD DOUGLAS

Letter to Douglass' Monthly

January 8, 1863

H. Ford Douglas, no relation to Frederick Douglass (writers sometimes mistakenly added an extra "s" to his last name), had escaped from slavery in 1846 and become an abolitionist speaker and writer. In July 1862, he became one of the few African Americans enlisted in a white regiment, the Ninety-fifth Illinois Volunteer Infantry. While stationed at Colliersville, Tennessee, he wrote a letter to Douglass's magazine, expressing

From H. Ford Douglas to *Douglass' Monthly*, January 8, 1863, in *Douglass' Monthly*, February 1863, 786.

the importance of coupling black enlistment to the Emancipation Proclamation.

The slaves are *free*! And how can I write these precious words? And yet it is so unless twenty millions of people cradled in christianity and civilization for a thousand years commits the foulest perjury that ever blackened the pages of history. In anticipation of this result I enlisted six Months ago in order to be better prepared to play my part in the great drama of the Negroe's redemption. I wanted its drill, its practical details for mere theory does not make a good soldier. I have learned something of war for I have seen war in its brightest as well as its bloodiest phase and yet I have nothing to regret. For since the stern necessities of this struggle have laid bare the naked issue of freedom on one side and slavery on the other — freedom shall have in the future of this conflict if necessary my blood as it has had in the past my earnest and best words. It seems to me that you can have no good reason for withholding from the government your hearty co operation. This war will educate Mr Lincoln out of his idea of the deportation of the Negro quite as fast as it has some of his other pro slavery ideas with respect to employing them as soldiers.

28

FREDERICK DOUGLASS

"Men of Color, to Arms!"

March 2, 1863

Black enlistment became the leading cause of Frederick Douglass in 1863. In March, he published "Men of Color, to Arms!" in his magazine, Douglass' Monthly, *dating the editorial March 2, 1863. He reprinted or spoke versions of the essay on many occasions afterward. The phrase "Men of Color, to Arms!" became a rallying cry for African American recruiters and enlistees. Two of Douglass's sons joined the Fifty-fourth*

From Frederick Douglass, "Men of Color, to Arms!" *Douglass' Monthly*, March 1863, 801.

Massachusetts Volunteer Infantry, a black regiment authorized by Governor John A. Andrew and eventually commanded by Robert Gould Shaw, the son of prominent white abolitionists. Douglass's editorial mentions the prospect of equal pay for black soldiers. He did not yet know that they would be paid less. Once he learned of the policy, he and other antislavery leaders, as well as black soldiers themselves, fought successfully for equal pay. Douglass even had a private meeting with Lincoln—the first of three private conversations that he would have with the president during the war—to discuss the issue of pay as well as other matters regarding African Americans in the military.

When first the rebel cannon shattered the walls of Sumter . . . I predicted that the war then and there inaugurated would not be fought out entirely by white men. Every month's experience during these two dreary years, has confirmed that opinion. A war undertaken and brazenly carried on, for the perpetual enslavement of colored men, calls logically and loudly upon colored men to help to suppress it. Only a moderate share of sagacity was needed to see that the arm of the slave was the best defense against the arm of the slaveholder. Hence, with every reverse to the national arms, with every exulting shout of victory raised by the slaveholding rebels, I have implored the imperilled nation to unchain against her foes her powerful black hand. Slowly and reluctantly that appeal is beginning to be heeded. . . . There is no time for delay. The tide is at its flood that leads on to fortune. From East to West, from North to South, the sky is written all over "NOW OR NEVER!" Liberty won for us by white men would lack half its lustre. "Who would be free themselves must strike the blow." Better even to die free than to live slaves. This is the sentiment of every brave colored man amongst us. There are weak and cowardly men in all nations. We have them amongst us. They will tell you that this is the "white man's war," that you will be "no better off after than before the war," that the object of getting you into the army is to "sacrifice you on the first opportunity." Believe them not. Cowards themselves, they do not wish to have their cowardice shamed by your brave example. Leave them to their timidity—or to whatever motive may hold them back. . . .

Massachusetts now welcomes you to arms as her soldiers. She has but a small colored population from which to recruit. She has full leave of the General Government to send one regiment to the war, and she has undertaken to do it. Go quickly and help fill up this first colored regiment from the North. I am authorized to assure you that you will receive the same wages, the same rations, the same equipments, the same protection, the same treatment, and the same bounty secured to white soldiers. You will be led by able and skillful officers, men who will take special pride in your efficiency and success. They will be quick to accord to you all the honor you shall merit by your valor, and see that your rights and feelings are respected by other soldiers. . . .

The day dawns. The morning star is bright upon the horizon. The iron gate of our prison stands half open. One gallant rush from the North will fling it wide open, while four millions of our brothers and sisters shall march out into liberty!

29

SATTIE A. DOUGLAS

Letter to the Anglo-African

June 9, 1863

Sattira A. Douglas of Massachusetts was the wife of H. Ford Douglas (see Document 27), who in June 1863 was still serving in the Ninety-fifth Illinois Volunteer Infantry. The Anglo-African, *a weekly black newspaper published in New York City, mistakenly listed her as "Sattie A. Douglass."*

It is true that now is offered the only opportunity that will be extended, during the present generation, for colored men to strike the blow that will at once relieve them of northern prejudice and southern slavery. If they do not now enroll among those other noble men who have gone forth to do battle for the true and right, it will only prove the correctness of the aspersion indulged in by our enemies, that we are unworthy of those rights which they have so long withheld from us, and that freedom would not be appreciated by us, if possessed.

It is no less true of nations than of individuals, that that which is the most dearly bought is the most highly prized, and the liberty, which we sacrifice our all to obtain, will be proportionately appreciated. This

From Sattie A. Douglas, letter to the editor, June 9, 1863, in *Anglo-African*, June 20, 1863.

revolution, like all others, is to act as a national purifier. We are now undergoing a process of fermentation, and all those false and unwholesome theories which have and do possess the American mind in regard to the relation which the colored race is to sustain towards the other nations of the world, are to work to the surface and pass off. This war is also to act as an educator, not only national, but individual. It is to teach us, regardless of sex or complexion, hard lessons of sacrifice, of courage, and of fortitude. . . . Colored men have everything to gain in this conflict: liberty, honor, social and political position are now placed within their grasp. They have these on the one side, and on the other slavery, prejudice of caste, and all other attendant evils.

The men who have been freed by the Proclamation seem generally to understand what is required of them, from their willingness to enlist. . . . [They] swell the ranks of dark-hued but determined avengers, whose destination is the far South.

30

HANNAH JOHNSON

Letter to Abraham Lincoln

July 31, 1863

On July 18, 1863, the Fifty-fourth Massachusetts attacked Fort Wagner, one of the batteries protecting Charleston Harbor. The engagement led to the single greatest day of losses for the regiment: More than 100 men were killed, and another 156 were wounded or captured. African American prisoners of war faced the prospect of death because of the Confederate policy, announced by Jefferson Davis in December 1862, that black Union soldiers would be treated as armed slaves in insurrection — they could be punished by death. In fact, the Confederate military authorities had a reason not to execute black prisoners: If kept alive, they could be exchanged for Confederate prisoners. Hannah Johnson of Buffalo, New York, was one of many people who pleaded with President Lincoln to do something about the Confederate policy regarding black prisoners. Johnson was

Hannah Johnson to Abraham Lincoln, July 31, 1863, RG 94, ser. 360, Records of the Adjutant General's Office, Colored Troops Division, Letters Received, file J-17 (1863), National Archives, Washington, D.C.

unaware that the day before she wrote her letter, Lincoln had issued General Order 252, which protested against the policy and announced that the Union would execute one Confederate prisoner for every Union prisoner, black or white, killed by the Confederacy. There is no evidence that Lincoln read Johnson's letter. He did not reply.

Excellent Sir

My good friend says I must write to you and she will send it. My son went in the 54th regiment. I am a colored woman and my son was strong and able as any to fight for his country and the colored people have as much to fight for as any. My father was a Slave and escaped from Louisiana before I was born forty years agone. I have but poor edication but I never went to schol, but I know just as well as any what is right between man and man. Now I know it is right that a colored man should go and fight for his country, and so ought to a white man. I know that a colored man ought to run no greater risques than a white, his pay is no greater[,] his obligation to fight is the same. So why should not our enemies be compelled to treat him the same, made to do it.

My son fought at Fort Wagoner but thank God he was not taken prisoner, as many were. I thought of this thing before I let my boy go but they said Mr. Lincoln will never let them sell our colored soldiers for slaves, if they do he will get them back quick[,] he will rettallyate and stop it. Now Mr Lincoln don't you think you ought to stop this thing and make them do the same by the colored men[;] they have lived in idleness all their lives on stolen labor and made savages of the colored people, but they are so furious because they are proving themselves to be men, such as have come away and got some edication. It must not be so. You must put the rebels to work in State prisons to making shoes and things, if they sell our colored soldiers, till they let them all go. And give their wounded the same treatment. It would seem cruel, but their no other way, and a just man must do hard things sometimes, and shew him to be a great man. They tell me some do you will take back the Proclamation, don't do it. When you are dead and in Heaven, in a thousand years that action of yours will make the angels sing your praises I know it. Ought one man to own another, law for or not, who made the law, surely the poor slave did not. So it is wicked, and a horrible Outrage, there is no sense in it, because a man has lived by robbing all his life and his father before him, should he complain because the stolen things found on him are taken. Robbing the colored people of their labor is but a small part of the robbery[;] their souls are almost taken, they are made bruits of often. You know all about this[.]

Will you see that the colored men fighting now, are fairly treated. You ought to do this and do it at once, Not let the thing run along[,] meet it quickly and manfully, and stop this, mean cowardly cruelty. We poor oppressed ones, appeal to you, and ask fair play.

Yours for Christs sake
Hannah Johnson

31

MARTHA GLOVER

Letter to Richard Glover
December 30, 1863

Slaves who wanted to join the Union army stood a better chance of escaping successfully if they fled alone rather than with their families. However, leaving relatives behind meant risking their punishment by irate masters. As a result, slaves who escaped to Union lines often guided forces to their old homes to liberate their wives and children, who were already declared free by the Emancipation Proclamation. But in the Border States, where the Proclamation was not in effect, families of escaped slaves now serving as soldiers were technically still enslaved and thus especially vulnerable to extended abuse by their masters. Martha Glover, from the town of Mexico in the Border State of Missouri, described her treatment to her husband, who was serving in the Union army. Soon after she wrote the letter, her master tried to move her and three of her children to Kentucky, but a Union officer kept him from doing so. Not until March 1865 did Congress pass a law freeing the wives and children of black soldiers, including those in the Border States.

My Dear Husband

I have received your last kind letter a few days ago and was much pleased to hear from you once more. It seems like a long time since you left me. I have had nothing but trouble since you left. You recollect

Martha Glover to Richard Glover, December 30, 1863, RG 393, ser. 2593, Department of Missouri, file P-91 (1864), National Archives, Washington, D.C.

what I told you how they would do after you was gone. They abuse me
because you went & say they will not take care of our children & do
nothing but quarrel with me all the time and beat me scandalously the
day before yesterday—Oh I never thought you would give me so much
trouble as I have got to bear now. You ought not to have left me in the fix
I am in & all these little helpless children to take care of. I was invited to
a party to night but I could not go[.] I am in too much trouble to want to
go to parties. The children talk about you all the time. I wish you could
get a furlough and come to see us once more. We want to see you worse
than we ever did before. Remember all I told you about how they would
do me after you left—for they do worse than they ever did. I do not
know what will become of me & my poor little children. Oh I wish you
had staid with me & not gone till I could go with you for I do nothing but
grieve about you. Write & tell me when you are coming.

Tell Isaac that his mother come & got his clothes[;] she was so sorry
he went. You need not tell me to beg any more married men to go. I see
too much trouble to try to get any more into trouble—too—Write to
me & do not forget me & my children[.]

farewell my dear husband
from your wife Martha

32

CHARLOTTE FORTEN

Life on the Sea Islands

June 1864

*Charlotte Forten was born in 1837 in Philadelphia. Her father and
mother, both members of prominent African American families, sent her
to school in Massachusetts, where she eventually became a teacher. In
late 1862, Forten joined other teachers on a journey to the Sea Islands
of South Carolina, where they taught young freed people. She regularly
wrote in her journal, providing one of the best records of events in the
Union-occupied low country during the Civil War. Forten witnessed the
creation of black schools, the transition from slave labor to wage labor in*

From Charlotte Forten, "Life on the Sea Islands," *Atlantic Monthly*, June 1864, 668–70.

the fields, and the arrival of African American regiments. On January 1, 1863, public readings of the Emancipation Proclamation took place throughout the region. On the anniversary of the Proclamation a year later, the freed people celebrated again. Here Forten describes the commemoration, as well as some of the black soldiers' encampments. Among the people she mentions are the northerners Colonel Thomas Wentworth Higginson, commander of the First South Carolina Volunteers, a black regiment; Reverend Mansfield French, an army chaplain who advocated landownership for African Americans; and Frances Gage, a superintendent of the freedmen and a longtime reformer and antislavery activist.

New-Year's Day—Emancipation Day—was a glorious one to us. The morning was quite cold, the coldest we had experienced; but we were determined to go to the celebration at Camp Saxton,—the camp of the First Regiment South-Carolina Volunteers,—whither the General and Colonel Higginson had bidden us, on this, "the greatest day in the nation's history." . . . [At Camp Saxton] everything looked clean and comfortable, much neater, we were told, than in most of the white camps. An officer told us that he had never seen a regiment in which the men were so honest. "In many other camps," said he, "the colonel and the rest of us would find it necessary to place a guard before our tents. We never do it here. They are left entirely unguarded. Yet nothing has ever been touched." We were glad to know that. It is a remarkable fact, when we consider that these men have all their lives been *slaves*; and we know what the teachings of Slavery are.

The celebration took place in the . . . largest grove we had seen. . . . There were the black soldiers in their blue coats and scarlet pantaloons, the officers of this and other regiments in their handsome uniforms, and crowds of lookers-on—men, women, and children, of every complexion, grouped in various attitudes under the moss-hung trees. The faces of all wore a happy, interested look. The exercises commenced with a prayer by the chaplain of the regiment. An ode, written for the occasion by Professor Zachos, was read by him, and then sung. Colonel Higginson then introduced Dr. Brisbane, who read the President's Proclamation, which was enthusiastically cheered. Rev. Mr. French presented to the Colonel two very elegant flags, a gift to the regiment from the Church of the Puritans, accompanying them by an appropriate and enthusiastic speech. At its conclusion, before Colonel Higginson could reply, and while he still stood holding the flag in his hand, some of the colored people commenced singing, "My Country, 'tis of thee." It was a touching and beautiful incident, and sent a thrill through all our hearts.

He said that that reply was far more effective than any speech he could make. But he did make one of those stirring speeches which are "half battles." All hearts swelled with emotion as we listened to his glorious words,—"stirring the soul like the sound of a trumpet." . . .

Mrs. Gage also uttered some earnest words; and then the regiment sang "John Brown" with much spirit. After the meeting we saw the dress-parade, a brilliant and beautiful sight. An officer told us that the men went through the drill remarkably well,—that the ease and rapidity with which they learned the movements were wonderful. To us it seemed as strange as a miracle,—this black regiment, the first mustered into the service of the United States, doing itself honor in the sight of the other regiments, many of whom, doubtless, "came to scoff." . . .

Our hearts were filled with an exceeding great gladness; for, although the Government had left much undone, we knew that Freedom was surely born in our land that day. It seemed too glorious a good to realize,—this the beginning of the great work we had so longed and prayed for.

33

GEORGE E. STEPHENS

The Pay of Colored Troops

August 1, 1864

George E. Stephens was perhaps the most influential black newspaper correspondent during the Civil War. A regular contributor to the Anglo-African, *Stephens traveled with many black regiments, including the Fifty-fourth Massachusetts. His reports from the front provided some of the most detailed and accurate accounts of the African American military experience. He was not hesitant about offering his opinions, including his criticism of the poor pay for black Union soldiers. Throughout 1863 and early 1864, African American soldiers continued to be paid only ten dollars per month, three dollars less than white soldiers earned, and some received as little as seven dollars per month. Worse, the War Department was slow in paying black troops, many of whom served for months*

From George E. Stephens, "The Pay of Colored Troops," August 1, 1864, in *Anglo-African*, August 27, 1864.

*without receiving any back pay. Protest and even mutiny resulted in some
black regiments. Finally, on June 15, 1864, Congress passed a law giving
all black soldiers pay. The law maintained a disparity based on time of
emancipation, however: Those black soldiers who could prove that they
were already free as of April 19, 1861, were to be paid retroactively to the
time of their enlistment, whereas those who were enslaved at that time
were to be paid retroactively only to January 1, 1864. The War Department also continued to be slow in providing back pay to black soldiers.*

Two or three months ago, it was announced that Congress had passed a
law equalizing the pay of colored troops. This was at the closing period
of the session. The colored troops which had been enlisted under the
law of 1862, were unpaid. . . . The War Department . . . refused to pay
soldiers who had black skins more than seven dollars per month.

Thus free men were reduced to servitude. No matter what services
he might render—no matter how nobly he might acquit himself—he
must carry with him the degradation of not being considered a man, but
a thing. The foreigner, the alien, of whatever color, or race, or country,
are enrolled and paid like native Americans; but the latest refinement of
cruelty has been brought to bear on us.

In the Revolutionary War, and in the War of 1812, colored men fought,
and were enrolled, and paid, the same as whites; and not only this, were
drilled and enlisted indiscriminately in the same companies and regiments. Little did our forefathers think that they were forging chains for
the limbs of their own race. . . .

Does the Lincoln despotism think it can succeed? There are those
who say, you should not talk so—"you hurt yourself." Let me say to
those men, we cannot be injured more. There is no insult—there is no
cruelty—there is no wrong, which we have not suffered. Torture, massacre, mobs, and slavery. Do you think that we will tamely submit like
spaniels to every indignity?

I shall speak hereafter my wrongs, and nothing shall prevent me but
double irons or a pistol-ball that shall take me out of the hell I am now
suffering: Nearly eighteen months of service—of labor—of humilia-
tion—of danger, and not one dollar. An estimable wife reduced to beg-
gary, and dependent upon another man—what can wipe out the wrong
and insult this Lincoln despotism has put upon us? . . . Who would have
believed that all the newspaper talk of the pay of colored soldiers having
been settled by Congress was a base falsehood. There is not the least
sign of pay, and there are hints from those in authority that we will not

get paid, and will be held to service by the terrors of our own bullets. Seventeen months and upwards! Suppose we had been white? Massachusetts would have inaugurated a rebellion in the East, and we would have been paid. But—Oh, how insulting!—because I am black, they tamper with my rights. How dare I be offered half the pay of any man, be he white or red.

34

SPOTSWOOD RICE

Letter to Kitty Diggs

September 3, 1864

Although the Militia Act of 1862 freed black soldiers' wives and children belonging to owners in rebellion, Congress failed to extend the act to the Border States until March 1865. The delay did not stop some black soldiers, such as Spotswood Rice, from using their new power to liberate family members by force. Rice and his family had been owned by Kitty Diggs of St. Louis, who rented out many of Rice's family members to work in the country outside St. Louis.[1] In a letter to his children, Rice wrote that he was heading up the Missouri River with a huge army and would soon set them free. He had lost his "sympathy for slaveholders," he told them, and he denied Diggs's claim that he had no right to "steal" his children from her. "You tell her from me," he wrote, "that she is the first Christian that I ever heard say that a man [sic] could steal his own child especially out of human bondage."[2] In a separate letter, Rice addressed Diggs directly.

---

[1] See the narrative of Mary A. Bell, Spotswood Rice's daughter, "She Loves Army Men," in *The American Slave: A Composite Autobiography*, ed. George P. Rawick, vol. 11, *Arkansas Narratives, Part 7, and Missouri Narratives* (1941; repr., Westport, Conn.: Greenwood, 1972), 25–31.

[2] Spotswood Rice to "My Children," September 3, 1864, enclosed in F. W. Diggs to William S. Rosecrans, September 10, 1864, RG 393, ser. 2593, Department of Missouri, file D-296 (1864), National Archives, Washington, D.C.

Spotswood Rice to Kitty Diggs, n.d., enclosed in F. W. Diggs to William S. Rosecrans, September 10, 1864, RG 393, ser. 2593, Department of Missouri, file D-296 (1864), National Archives, Washington, D.C.

I received a letter . . . telling me that you say I tried to steal to plunder my child away from you now I want you to understand that mary is my Child and she is a God given rite of my own and you may hold on to her as long as you can but I want you to remembor this one thing that the longor you keep my child from me the longor you will have to burn in hell and the qwicer you'll get their for we are now makeing up about one thoughsande black troops to come up tharough and wont to come through Glasgow[3] and when we come wo be to Copperhood rabbels[4] and to the slaveholding rebbels for we don't expect to leave them. . . . I want you to understand kittey diggs that where ever you and I meets we are enmays to each orthere I offered once to pay you forty dollers for my own Child but I am glad now that you did not accept it. . . . My Children is my own and I expect to get them and when I get ready to come after mary I will have bout a powrer and autherity to bring hear away and to exacute vengencens on them that holds my Child. . . . I have no fears about getting mary out of your hands this whole Government gives chear to me and you cannot help your self.

5

The Confederacy Considers Emancipation

At the start of the Civil War, most Confederates would have found it inconceivable that the new nation would ever emancipate slaves. After all, Alexander H. Stephens had declared slavery the cornerstone of the Confederacy (Document 4). Even those who supported the idea of letting slaves fight for the Confederacy thought they might do so without any promise of freedom in exchange (Document 6).

Yet as the Confederate war effort began to falter in late 1863 and early 1864, more southern whites began to take seriously the idea of promising slaves their freedom in exchange for their service in the Confederate army. Such a scheme seemed reasonable in light of the apparent willingness of some free African Americans to fight for the Confederacy at the start of the war. The Louisiana Native Guards, for example, had formed their own unit in late 1861 and volunteered to join the Confederacy, although the Confederacy never mustered them into the army, and some of them eventually joined the Union army. Southern whites' doubts about African Americans' courage in battle had weakened as blacks in Union uniform had succeeded in numerous military engagements. Also, in a series of speeches in late 1864, President Jefferson Davis, in an attempt to bolster Confederate nationalism, had declared that the cause of the war was national independence more than the survival of slavery.

Within months of the Emancipation Proclamation, Confederate officers and civilian leaders began talking in earnest about the possibility of emancipating and enlisting slaves (Documents 35, 37, and 39). But opposition to the idea was massive and fierce right to the end of the war (Documents 36 and 38), and southern whites seemed more willing to enlist teenagers and old men before they would give guns and Confederate uniforms to slaves. Although a small number of African Americans did end up serving as Confederate soldiers at the very end of the war, none ever saw combat.

35

PATRICK R. CLEBURNE

Letter to the Commanders of the Army of the Tennessee

January 2, 1864

On their own initiative, Confederate General Patrick R. Cleburne and thirteen other officers of the Army of the Tennessee wrote a letter to the commanders of the Confederate army recommending the emancipation and enlistment of African Americans. President Davis was furious when he found out about the letter, ordered it suppressed, and prohibited further discussion of the proposal.

We have now been fighting for nearly three years, have spilled much of our best blood, and lost, consumed, or thrown to the flames an amount of property equal in value to the specie currency of the world. Through some lack in our system the fruits of our struggles and sacrifices have invariably slipped away from us and left us nothing but long lists of dead and mangled. Instead of standing defiantly on the borders of our territory or harassing those of the enemy, we are hemmed in to-day into less than two-thirds of it, and still the enemy menacingly confronts us at every point with superior forces. Our soldiers can see no end to this state of affairs except in our own exhaustion; hence, instead of rising to the occasion, they are sinking into a fatal apathy, growing weary of hardships and slaughters which promise no results. . . . If this state continues much longer we must be subjugated. Every man should endeavor to understand the meaning of subjugation before it is too late. . . . It means the loss of all we now hold most sacred — slaves and all other personal property, lands, homesteads, liberty, justice, safety, pride, manhood. It means that the history of this heroic struggle will be written by the enemy; that our youth will be trained by Northern school teachers; will learn from Northern school books their version of the war; will be

From *War of the Rebellion: The Official Records of the Union and Confederate Armies* (Washington, D.C.: Government Printing Office, 1898), ser. 1, 52, pt. 2:586–92.

impressed by all the influences of history and education to regard our gallant dead as traitors, our maimed veterans as fit objects for derision. It means the crushing of Southern manhood, the hatred of our former slaves, who will, on a spy system, be our secret police. The conqueror's policy is to divide the conquered into factions and stir up animosity among them, and in training an army of negroes the North no doubt holds this thought in perspective. . . .

Our single source of supply is that portion of our white men fit for duty and not now in the ranks. The enemy has three sources of supply: First, his own motley population; secondly, our slaves; and thirdly, Europeans whose hearts are fired into a crusade against us by fictitious pictures of the atrocities of slavery, and who meet no hindrance from their Governments in such enterprise, because these Governments are equally antagonistic to the institution. . . . Apart from the assistance that home and foreign prejudice against slavery has given to the North, slavery is a source of great strength to the enemy in a purely military point of view, by supplying him with an army from our granaries; but it is our most vulnerable point, a continued embarrassment, and in some respects an insidious weakness. . . . All along the lines slavery is comparatively valueless to us for labor, but of great and increasing worth to the enemy for information. It is an omnipresent spy system, pointing out our valuable men to the enemy, revealing our positions, purposes, and resources, and yet acting so safely and secretly that there is no means to guard against it. . . .

In view of the state of affairs what does our country propose to do? . . . We propose . . . that we retain in service for the war all troops now in service, and that we immediately commence training a large reserve of the most courageous of our slaves, and further that we guarantee freedom within a reasonable time to every slave in the South who shall remain true to the Confederacy in this war. As between the loss of independence and the loss of slavery, we assume that every patriot will freely give up the latter—give up the negro slave rather than be a slave himself. If we are correct in this assumption it only remains to show how this great national sacrifice is, in all human probabilities, to change the current of success and sweep the invader from our country. . . .

. . . This measure will deprive the North of the moral and material aid which it now derives from the bitter prejudices with which foreigners view the institution, and its war, if continued, will henceforth be so despicable in their eyes that the source of recruiting will be dried up. It will leave the enemy's negro army no motive to fight for, and will exhaust the source from which it has been recruited. The idea that it is their special mission to war against slavery has held growing sway over the Northern people for many years, and has at length ripened into an armed and bloody crusade against it. This baleful superstition has so far supplied them with a courage and constancy not their own. . . . The measure we propose will strike dead all John Brown fanaticism, and will compel the enemy to draw off altogether or in the eyes of the world to swallow the Declaration of Independence without the sauce and disguise of philanthropy. . . .

Apart from all other aspects of the question, the necessity for more fighting men is upon us. We can only get a sufficiency by making the negro share the danger and hardships of the war. If we arm and train him and make him fight for the country in her hour of dire distress, every consideration of principle and policy demand that we should set him and his whole race who side with us free. It is a first principle with mankind that he who offers his life in defense of the State should receive from her in return his freedom and his happiness, and we believe in acknowledgment of this principle. . . . The hope of freedom is perhaps the only moral incentive that can be applied to him in his present condition. It would be preposterous then to expect him to fight against it with any degree of enthusiasm, therefore we must bind him to our cause by no doubtful bonds; we must leave no possible loop-hole for treachery to creep in. The slaves are dangerous now, but armed, trained, and collected in an army they would be a thousand fold more dangerous: therefore when we make soldiers of them we must make free men of them beyond all question, and thus enlist their sympathies also. We can do this more effectually than the North can now do, for we can give the negro not only his own freedom, but that of his wife and child, and can secure it to him in his old home.[1] To do this, we must immediately make his marriage and parental relations sacred in the eyes of the law and forbid their sale. . . . Satisfy the negro that if he faithfully adheres to our standard during the war he shall receive his freedom and that of his race. Give him as an earnest of our intentions such immediate immunities as will impress him with our sincerity and be in keeping with his new condition, enroll a portion of his class as soldiers of the Confederacy, and we change the race from a dreaded weakness to a position of strength.

---

[1] By the time of this letter, the Union had passed legislation emancipating the families of former slaves from rebellious areas who served in the armed forces, but this measure was not extended to the Border States until early 1865.

Will the slaves fight? . . . The negro slaves of Saint Domingo, fighting for freedom, defeated their white masters and the French troops sent against them. . . .[2]

. . . It is said slavery is all we are fighting for, and if we give it up we give up all. Even if this were true, which we deny, slavery is not all our enemies are fighting for. It is merely the pretense to establish sectional superiority and a more centralized form of government, and to deprive us of our rights and liberties. We have now briefly proposed a plan which we believe will save our country. It may be imperfect, but in all human probability it would give us our independence. No objection ought to outweigh it which is not weightier than independence.

[2] Santo Domingo, or St. Domingo, was the name nineteenth-century orators and writers often used to refer to St. Domingue, the French colony on the western side of the island now known as Hispaniola. In 1791, a slave revolt there led to the creation of the independent country of Haiti.

36

CONGRESS OF THE CONFEDERATE STATES OF AMERICA

Address to the People of the Confederate States
January 22, 1864

To show a united front against emancipation, and against ideas such as General Patrick R. Cleburne's (Document 35), the Confederate Congress issued a joint resolution, signed by all members of both houses, linking the preservation of slavery with the welfare of the Confederacy.

Resolved by the Congress of the Confederate States of America, That the present is deemed a fitting occasion to remind the people of the Confederate States that they are engaged in a struggle for the preservation both of liberty and civilization; and that no sacrifice of life or fortune can

From *War of the Rebellion: The Official Records of the Union and Confederate Armies* (Washington, D.C.: Government Printing Office, 1880), ser. 4, 3:126–27, 132–34.

be too costly which may be requisite to secure to themselves and their posterity the enjoyment of these inappreciable blessings. . . .

Compelled, by a long series of oppressive and tyrannical acts, culminating at last in the selection of a President and Vice-President, by a party confessedly sectional and hostile to the South and her institutions, these States withdrew from the former Union and formed a new Confederate alliance as an independent Government, based on the proper relations of labor and capital. This step was taken reluctantly, by constraint, and after the exhaustion of every measure that was likely to secure us from interference with our property, equality in the Union, or exemption from submission to an alien Government. The Southern States claimed only the unrestricted enjoyment of the rights guaranteed by the Constitution. Finding, by painful and protracted experience, that this was persistently denied, we determined to separate from those enemies who had manifested the inclination and ability to impoverish and destroy us. We fell back upon the right for which the Colonies maintained the war of the Revolution, and which our heroic forefathers asserted to be clear and inalienable. . . .

. . . Cruelties and atrocities of the enemy have been exceeded by their malicious and bloodthirsty purposes and machinations in reference to the slaves. Early in this war President Lincoln averred his constitutional inability and personal unwillingness to interfere with the domestic institutions of the States and the relation between master and servant. . . .

Subsequent reverses and the refractory rebelliousness of the seceded States caused a change of policy, and Mr. Lincoln issued his celebrated proclamation . . . liberating the slaves in the "insurrectionary districts.". . .

Disregarding the teachings of the approved writers on international law, and the practice and claims of his own Government in its purer days, President Lincoln has sought to convert the South into a San Domingo, by appealing to the cupidity, lusts, ambition, and ferocity of the slave. . . .

Subjugation involves everything that the torturing malice and devilish ingenuity of our foes can suggest—the destruction of our nationality, the equalization of whites and blacks, the obliteration of State lines, degradation to colonial vassalage, and the reduction of many of our citizens to dreary, hopeless, remediless bondage.

37

ROBERT E. LEE

Letter to Andrew Hunter
January 11, 1865

Jefferson Davis remained steadfast in his opposition to Confederate emancipation through 1864, arguing, among other things, that only the states, not the Confederate nation, could emancipate. On January 7, 1865, Andrew Hunter, a member of the Virginia state senate, wrote to General Robert E. Lee that the states might soon have to take up the question of emancipating and enlisting slaves. Hunter favored emancipation, though he was concerned about the "mountain of prejudice growing out of our ancient modes of regarding the institution of Southern slavery."[3] He asked Lee for his opinion. Lee answered the letter, and his opinion in favor of emancipation was soon known to all in the Confederate high command, including President Davis.

Considering the relation of master and slave, controlled by humane laws and influenced by Christianity and an enlightened public sentiment, as the best that can exist between the white and black races while intermingled as at present in this country, I would deprecate any sudden disturbance of that relation unless it be necessary to avert a greater calamity to both. I should therefore prefer to rely upon our white population to preserve the ratio between our forces and those of the enemy, which experience has shown to be safe. But in view of the preparations of our enemies, it is our duty to provide for continued war and not for a battle or a campaign, and I fear that we cannot accomplish this without overtaxing the capacity of our white population.

Should the war continue under the existing circumstances, the enemy may in course of time penetrate our country and get access to a large part of our negro population. It is his avowed policy to convert the able-bodied men among them into soldiers, and to emancipate all.... I

[3] "Memoranda on the Civil War," *Century Magazine*, August 1888, 599.

From *War of the Rebellion: The Official Records of the Union and Confederate Armies* (Washington, D.C.: Government Printing Office, 1880), ser. 4, 3:1012–13.

think, therefore, we must decide whether slavery shall be extinguished by our enemies and the slaves be used against us, or use them ourselves at the risk of the effects which must be produced upon our social institutions. My opinion is that we should employ them without delay. I believe that with proper regulations they can be made efficient soldiers. They possess the physical qualifications in an eminent degree. Long habits of obedience and subordination, coupled with the moral influence which in our country the white man possesses over the black, furnish an excellent foundation for that discipline which is the best guaranty of military efficiency. Our chief aim should be to secure their fidelity.

There have been formidable armies composed of men having no interest in the cause for which they fought beyond their pay or the hope of plunder. But it is certain that the surest foundation upon which the fidelity of an army can rest, especially in a service which imposes peculiar hardships and privations, is the personal interest of the soldier in the issue of the contest. Such an interest we can give our negroes by giving immediate freedom to all who enlist, and freedom at the end of the war to the families of those who discharge their duties faithfully (whether they survive or not), together with the privilege of residing at the South. To this might be added a bounty for faithful service.

We should not expect slaves to fight for prospective freedom when they can secure it at once by going to the enemy, in whose service they will incur no greater risk than in ours. The reasons that induce me to recommend the employment of negro troops at all render the effect of the measures I have suggested upon slavery immaterial, and in my opinion the best means of securing the efficiency and fidelity of this auxiliary force would be to accompany the measure with a well-digested plan of gradual and general emancipation. As that will be the result of the continuance of the war, and will certainly occur if the enemy succeed, it seems to me most advisable to adopt it at once, and thereby obtain all the benefits that will accrue to our cause. . . .

In addition to the great political advantages that would result to our cause from the adoption of a system of emancipation, it would exercise a salutary influence upon our whole negro population, by rendering more secure the fidelity of those who become soldiers, and diminishing the inducements to the rest to abscond.

38

CHARLESTON MERCURY

Lunacy

January 13, 1865

As Virginia began to consider emancipating slaves and enlisting them in the military, many whites in the Deep South looked on with horror. The Charleston Mercury, *one of the most pro-secession and proslavery newspapers in the South, ridiculed Virginia.*

The wild talk prevalent in the official and the semi-official organs at Richmond grates harshly upon the ear of South Carolina. It is still more grievous to her to hear the same unmanly proposition from those in authority in the old State of Virginia. Side by side Carolina and Virginia have stood together against all comers for near two centuries—the exemplars and authors of Southern civilization. . . .

It was on account of encroachments upon the institution of *slavery* by the sectional majority of the old Union, that South Carolina seceded from that Union. It is not at this late day, after the loss of thirty thousand of her best and bravest men in battle, that she will suffer it to be bartered away; or ground between the upper and nether mill stones, by the madness of Congress, or the counsels of shallow men elsewhere.

By the compact we made with Virginia and the other States of this Confederacy, South Carolina will stand to the bitter end of destruction. By that compact she intends to stand or to fall. Neither Congress, nor certain make shift men in Virginia, can force upon her their mad schemes of weakness and surrender. She stands upon her institutions—and there she will fall in their defence. *We want no Confederate Government without our institutions.* . . . Thousands and tens of thousands of the bravest men, and the best blood of this State, fighting in the ranks, have left their bones whitening on the bleak hills of Virginia in this cause. We are fighting for our system of civilization. . . . The soldiers of South Carolina will not fight beside a nigger—to talk of emancipation is to disband our army. We are free men, and we chose to fight for ourselves—we want

From "Lunacy," *Charleston Mercury*, January 13, 1865.

no slaves to fight for us. Skulkers, money-lenders, money-makers, and blood-suckers, alone will tolerate the idea. It is the man who wont fight himself, who wants his nigger to fight for him, and to take his place in the ranks. Put that man in the ranks. And do it at once. . . . Falter and hack at the root of the Confederacy—our institutions—our civilization—and you kill the cause as dead as a boiled crab.

39

RICHMOND DAILY EXAMINER

Negro Troops
February 25, 1865

The Richmond Daily Examiner, *one of the leading papers in Virginia, joined with many state legislators in endorsing emancipation. With leading Virginians, including Robert E. Lee, in support of the proposal, Jefferson Davis finally relented. On March 13, 1865, he signed a law allowing slaves to be freed and to serve as soldiers, but only in states that had voted to approve emancipation and only if the slaves' owners had consented to the policy. By April 9, when Robert E. Lee surrendered to Ulysses S. Grant at Appomattox Court House, Virginia had created a few black companies, but they never saw military action.*

Undoubtedly the arming of negroes, whether as slaves or not, is a very serious step; justifies earnest deliberation, and accounts for honest differences of opinion. It is a great thing which General Lee asks us to do, and directly opposite to all the sentiments and principles which have heretofore governed the Southern people. . . .

The whole matter depends practically on the question—Is this necessary, or not necessary, to the defeat of the Yankee invaders and the establishment of Confederate independence? . . . As to those other and larger considerations, which do not depend upon military necessity, nor on the present exigency, but go down to the foundations of society and the natural relations of races, those Senators who hold that it would be a cruel injury, both to white and black, to sever their present relation of master and slave; that to make "freedom" a reward for service, is at war with the first principles of this relation, and is the beginning of abolition, and that abolition means the abandonment of the black race to inevitable destruction upon this continent, those Senators are undoubtedly right. This is the true Southern principle, and the only righteous principle. But what then? What good will our principle do if the Yankees come in over us? Will there be any comfort in going down to perdition carrying our principle with us intact? The principle of slavery is a sound one; but is it so dear to us that rather than give it up we would be slaves ourselves? Slavery, like the Sabbath, was made for man; not man for slavery.

6

Reconstruction Begins

Reconstruction began well before the Civil War ended. Opening military service to African Americans provided them with a sense and a reality of empowerment, but their precise political and legal status after the Emancipation Proclamation remained uncertain. Was the emancipation of all slaves ensured? President Lincoln called emancipation and black military service "the heaviest blow yet dealt to the rebellion," and despite the pressure he felt in the last years of the war to revoke the Emancipation Proclamation, he never seriously considered doing it. "If they stake their lives for us," Lincoln wrote of black soldiers, "they must be prompted by the strongest motive—even the promise of freedom. And the promise being made, must be kept."[1] But what sorts of measures would protect the freedom of African Americans? Would they have equal rights with white Americans? How would American society and government shape the transition from slave to free labor? All of these questions remained open long after emancipation became a clear war aim.

[1] Abraham Lincoln to James C. Conkling, August 26, 1863, in Roy P. Basler, ed., and Marion Dolores Pratt and Lloyd A. Dunlap, asst. eds., *The Collected Works of Abraham Lincoln* (New Brunswick, N.J.: Rutgers University Press, 1953–1955), 6:409.

40

HARRIET JACOBS

Letter to Lydia Maria Child
March 18, 1863

Harriet Jacobs was one of the best-known African American authors of the Civil War era. Writing under the pseudonym Linda Brent, she published Incidents in the Life of a Slave Girl *in 1861 with the encouragement and assistance of Lydia Maria Child, a white abolitionist and author (see Document 12). When the war began, Jacobs was working as a personal nurse in New York City, but she eventually traveled to work at Washington, D.C.'s "contraband camps," villages of freed people that sprang up when the war began and grew quickly after April 1862, when Congress abolished slavery in the city. Although the War Department appointed officers to oversee conditions in the camps, the lack of adequate housing, food, and water made life there challenging. Jacobs, who wrote to Child from a camp in Alexandria, Virginia, just outside Washington, D.C., had recently witnessed a smallpox outbreak, which had claimed the lives of hundreds of people in the area.*

Many [African American refugees] have found employment, and are supporting themselves and their families. It would do your heart good to talk with some of these people. They are quick, intelligent, and full of the spirit of freedom. Some of them say to me, "The white men of the North have helped us thus far, and we want to help *them*. We would like to fight for them, if they would only treat us like men." . . .

. . . Last night . . . our rough, little, poorly-built church . . . was densely crowded, and although some alarm was excited by the rafters giving way overhead, quiet was soon restored, and the people were deeply attentive. Eight couples were married on this occasion. We have a day-school of eighty scholars, and a large number attend our evening school—mostly adults. A large sewing-circle, composed of young and old, meets every Saturday afternoon. Three colored men teach a school in this city for those who can afford to pay somewhat for instruction. They have a large

From Harriet Jacobs to Lydia Maria Child, March 18, 1863, in *Liberator*, April 10, 1863.

number of pupils, mostly children of colored citizens; and a few of the "little contrabands" attend their school.

We are now collecting together the orphan children, of whom there are a great number, owing to the many deaths that have occurred of late. In justice to the refugee women, I am bound to testify that I have never known them, in one instance, refuse to shelter an orphan. In many cases, mothers who have five or six children of their own, without enough to feed and cover them, will readily receive these helpless little ones into their own poor hovels.

O, when will the white man learn to know the hearts of my abused and suffering people!

41

C. B. WILDER

Testimony before the American Freedmen's Inquiry Commission

May 9, 1863

Confronted by the question of what policies to create for African American civilians after the Emancipation Proclamation, the Lincoln administration created the American Freedmen's Inquiry Commission in March 1863. The three-person board interviewed former slaves as well as officials charged with supervising them. In May 1863, the board interviewed C. B. Wilder, the supervisor at Fortress Monroe in Virginia, where two years before General Benjamin Butler had held slaves as contraband of war (see Document 7).

Q: Is there any difference made between free black men and men made free by the proclamation?

From C. B. Wilder, Testimony before the American Freedmen's Inquiry Commission, May 9, 1863, RG 94, ser. 12, Records of the Adjutant General's Office, Letters Received, file O-328 (1863), National Archives, Washington, D.C.

A: Yes Sir[.] If there is a man who carries free papers they will give him a pass, to go to Baltimore or any where; but there is not one in 500 who have such papers. . . .

Q: In your opinion, is there any communication between the refugees and the black men still in slavery?

A: Yes Sir, we have had men here who have gone back 200 miles.

Q: In your opinion would a change in our policy which would cause them to be treated with fairness, their wages punctually paid and employment furnished them in the army, become known and would it have any effect upon others in slavery?

A: Yes. . . . The colored people actually sent a deputation to me . . . to know if we put black men in irons and sent them off to Cuba to be sold or set them at work and put balls on their legs and whipped them, just as in slavery; because that was the story up there, and they were frightened and didn't know what to do. When I got at the feelings of these people I found they were not afraid of the slaveholders. They said there was nobody on the plantations but women and they were not afraid of them. One woman came through 200 miles in Men's clothes. . . . I found hundreds who had left their wives and families behind. I asked them "Why did you come away and leave them there?" and I found they had heard these stories, and wanted to come and see how it was. "I am going back again after my wife" some of them said "When I have earned a little money." . . . "I am going for my family" they say. "Are you not afraid to risk it?" "No I know the Way." Colored men will help colored men and they will work along the paths and get through. . . . The white people have nearly all gone, the blood hounds are not there to hunt them and they are not afraid; before they were afraid to stir. . . .

Q: In your opinion do the intelligent planters in the neighborhood have any desire for the introduction of Northern labor here?

A: Sensible and intelligent men do. A great many have expressed that desire and they say the whole state will run out unless they have it. . . . Let these plantations be bought up for a small sum and parcelled off into lots of ten acres and let every black man have a little homestead of his own where he can live and go out to work. We are introducing cotton and tobacco here which will become a great source of revenue if we can retain the colored people here. I know men who will invest a hundred thousand dollars in the purchase of these plantations and cut them up into small homesteads for these people. We have got our schools all over this part of the country and are teaching them to read. We try to inspire them with the idea that they are to be free and that this is one of the conditions of freedom; and we tell them that when the war is over they can buy a spot of land, and have a little hut to live in with their families like everybody else.... [Before the war] I did not believe that one could make very much out of them. I did not think they had so much brain. They have got as many brains as you or I have, though they have an odd way of showing it. I have explained to them that if they expect freedom they must be worthy of it; that they must pack up every evil habit and be industrious, virtuous, and economical. Heretofore, they have always been driven to work, now our chief men will say they have never known men to work better.

42

NOYES WHEELER

The Riotous Outbreak in New York
July 20, 1863

From July 13 to 16, 1863, New York City was in chaos as mobs roamed the streets destroying civilian and military property and disrupting communication lines. The New York City draft riots, as they became known, were triggered by the attempted imposition of a draft in the city only days after newspapers reported the thousands of casualties at the Battle of Gettysburg, which took place from July 1 to 3. Frustrated at the prospect of further human losses and inflamed by political rhetoric that blamed Lincoln's demand for emancipation as the reason for the war's persistence, whites in the city set fire to African American boardinghouses and orphanages, attacked black soldiers, and lynched African American civilians. (Lynching would gain fame as a form of racial violence in the post–Civil War South, but it also existed before and during the war throughout the country.) Lincoln eventually had to order federal troops to quell the rioting in the city. Noyes Wheeler, one of the correspondents for the Liberator *in New York City, emphasized the violence against African Americans and white abolitionists like Horace Greeley in his report.*

From Noyes Wheeler, "The Riotous Outbreak in New York," letter to the editor, July 20, 1863, in *Liberator*, July 24, 1863.

In this city, during the past week, has been the reign of terror. . . .

Among the most cruel and barbarous acts of the mob was the slaughter of the colored people. In the evening, on Clarkson street, I saw a poor negro hanging by the neck on a tree. He was entirely naked, and a slow fire burning under him! His feet were partially roasted; his body scorched in several places, and lifeless! A crowd of low people, — men, women, and children, — were looking on; rude boys were poking the poor corpse with sticks, while others of the crowd were making derision of their victim.

A day or two afterwards, the mob hung another colored man on a tree, in Thirty-second street, not far from my office. It took place about six o'clock, A.M. Soon after it occurred, I ventured to go near the place of the horrible scene, and saw a most loathsome looking crowd, jeering at the mangled corpse as though they had done a worthy deed. They appeared more like demons than human beings. . . .

There were no policemen, no soldiers, on the ground. At last, the military came. . . . The cavalry with their swords cut down the dead body. It fell into the gutter: they left it lying there. The artillery soon fired their cannon, and raked the streets of the mob. After the military had left the scene, the rioters returned, and renewed their depredations. They hung up the dead carcass again, amid the cheers of howling demons. . . .

All Abolitionists and leading Republicans were in danger. Horace Greeley was called for by some of the mob.[2] They said they wanted to hang him by the side of the negro; and why they did not murder him, as he passed up and down regularly to his dinners and lodgings, is a miracle. The rioters threatened to burn every Anti-Slavery church, and kill every Abolitionist.

---

[2] Greeley was a well-known abolitionist and newspaper editor who had called for emancipation early in the war in his newspaper, the *New York Tribune* (see Document 14).

43

ABRAHAM LINCOLN

Gettysburg Address

November 19, 1863

Lincoln accepted an invitation to give a short address at the dedication of a national cemetery at the Gettysburg battlefield. Although his speech was not the featured address of the day—the major oration was the two-hour address given by the famous orator Edward Everett—Lincoln worked carefully on the text and continued to tinker with it even after he delivered it. Eventually, he drafted at least four versions. The version reprinted here, the only one Lincoln signed, is the "Bliss copy," so called because it was long owned by the Alexander Bliss family. Lincoln's attention to the speech reflected his understanding that he was declaring a new, higher meaning of the war. A poetic counterpart to the Emancipation Proclamation, the Gettysburg Address promised "a new birth of freedom," by which Lincoln meant not only reconstruction of the Union but universal emancipation as well. Yet he chose not to use the words slavery, abolition, *or* emancipation *in the speech. When the war was over, white Americans in particular came to prefer the Gettysburg Address to the Emancipation Proclamation, in part because the address treated freedom as an abstraction and did not mention the embarrassing institution of slavery. By the end of the nineteenth century, the Gettysburg Address had replaced the Emancipation Proclamation as the defining document of the Civil War.*

Four score and seven years ago our fathers brought forth on this continent a new nation, conceived in Liberty, and dedicated to the proposition that all men are created equal.

Now we are engaged in a great civil war, testing whether that nation, or any nation, so conceived and so dedicated, can long endure. We are met on a great battle-field of that war. We have come to dedicate a

From Roy P. Basler, ed., and Marion Dolores Pratt and Lloyd A. Dunlap, asst. eds., *The Collected Works of Abraham Lincoln* (New Brunswick, N.J.: Rutgers University Press, 1953–1955), 7:22–23.

portion of that field, as a final resting place for those who here gave their lives that that nation might live. It is altogether fitting and proper that we should do this.

But, in a larger sense, we can not dedicate—we can not consecrate—we can not hallow—this ground. The brave men, living and dead, who struggled here, have consecrated it, far above our poor power to add or detract. The world will little note, nor long remember what we say here, but it can never forget what they did here. It is for us the living, rather, to be dedicated here to the unfinished work which they who fought here have thus far so nobly advanced. It is rather for us to be here dedicated to the great task remaining before us—that from these honored dead we take increased devotion to that cause for which they gave the last full measure of devotion—that we here highly resolve that these dead shall not have died in vain—that this nation, under God, shall have a new birth of freedom—and that government of the people, by the people, for the people, shall not perish from the earth.

44

ANNIE DAVIS

Letter to Abraham Lincoln

August 25, 1864

More than a year and a half after Lincoln signed the Emancipation Proclamation, the legal status of slavery remained uncertain. Lincoln often said that the Proclamation, as a wartime measure, might be overturned by the Supreme Court or nullified by his successor in the White House. Also, slavery lived on in the Border States, which the Proclamation had exempted. No wonder, then, that Annie Davis, an African American from the Eastern Shore of Maryland but held in bondage in Bel Air, was unsure of her status when she wrote to Lincoln in August 1864. There

Annie Johnson to Abraham Lincoln, August 25, 1864, RG 94, ser. 360, Records of the Adjutant General's Office, Colored Troops Division, Letters Received, file D-304 (1864), National Archives, Washington, D.C.

is no evidence that Lincoln replied to Davis or even read her letter. One month after Davis wrote, Maryland voted to abolish slavery in the state.

Mr president

It is my Desire to be free. to go to see my people on the eastern shore. my mistress won't let me you will please let me know if we are free. and what I can do. I write to you for advice. please send me word this week. or as soon as possible and oblidge.

45

ABRAHAM LINCOLN

Second Inaugural

March 4, 1865

In November 1864, Lincoln won reelection. Soon after, he called for passage of the constitutional amendment abolishing slavery and cajoled individual congressmen to support the measure. On January 31, 1865, the House of Representatives passed the resolution for the amendment with the necessary two-thirds majority and sent it to the states for ratification. By the time of Lincoln's Second Inaugural, a number of states had ratified the amendment, including some of the seceded states that now were governed by Unionist legislatures. In accepting the votes of the Unionist legislatures in these states as legitimate, Lincoln revealed his belief that the states had never left the Union and that reconstruction should be speedy. Lincoln's Second Inaugural also carried a message of reconciliation, especially in its final paragraph. But the penultimate paragraph was much more gloomy and fatalistic. It echoed a letter he had written a year before to the Kentuckian Albert G. Hodges, which ended by saying, "I claim not to have controlled events, but confess plainly that events have controlled me. . . . If God now wills the removal of a great wrong, and wills also that we of the North as well as you of the South,

From Roy P. Basler, ed., and Marion Dolores Pratt and Lloyd A. Dunlap, asst. eds., *The Collected Works of Abraham Lincoln* (New Brunswick, N.J.: Rutgers University Press, 1953–1955), 8:332–33.

shall pay fairly for our complicity in that wrong, impartial history will find therein new cause to attest and revere the justice and goodness of God."[3]

Four years ago, all thoughts were anxiously directed to an impending civil-war. All dreaded it—all sought to avert it. . . . Both parties deprecated war; but one of them would *make* war rather than let the nation survive; and the other would *accept* war rather than let it perish. And the war came.

One eighth of the whole population were colored slaves, not distributed generally over the Union, but localized in the Southern part of it. These slaves constituted a peculiar and powerful interest. All knew that this interest was, somehow, the cause of the war. To strengthen, perpetuate, and extend this interest was the object for which the insurgents would rend the Union, even by war; while the government claimed no right to do more than to restrict the territorial enlargement of it. Neither party expected for the war, the magnitude, or the duration, which it has already attained. Neither anticipated that the *cause* of the conflict might cease with, or even before, the conflict itself should cease. Each looked for an easier triumph, and a result less fundamental and astounding. Both read the same Bible, and pray to the same God; and each invokes His aid against the other. It may seem strange that any men should dare to ask a just God's assistance in wringing their bread from the sweat of other men's faces; but let us judge not that we be not judged. The prayers of both could not be answered; that of neither has been answered fully. The Almighty has His own purposes. "Woe unto the world because of offences! for it must needs be that offences come; but woe to that man by whom the offence cometh!"[4] If we shall suppose that American Slavery is one of those offences which, in the providence of God, must needs come, but which, having continued through His appointed time, He now wills to remove, and that He gives to both North and South, this terrible war, as the woe due to those by whom the offence came, shall we discern therein any departure from those divine attributes which the believers in a Living God always ascribe to Him? Fondly do we hope—fervently do we pray—that this mighty scourge of war may speedily pass away. Yet, if God wills that it continue, until all the wealth piled by the bond-man's two hundred and fifty years of

[3] Roy P. Basler, ed., and Marion Dolores Pratt and Lloyd A. Dunlap, asst. eds., *The Collected Works of Abraham Lincoln* (New Brunswick, N.J.: Rutgers University Press, 1953–1955), 7:282.
[4] Matthew 18:17.

unrequited toil shall be sunk, and until every drop of blood drawn with the lash, shall be paid by another drawn with the sword, as was said three thousand years ago, so still it must be said "the judgments of the Lord, are true and righteous altogether."[5]

With malice toward none; with charity for all; with firmness in the right, as God gives us to see the right, let us strive on to finish the work we are in; to bind up the nation's wounds; to care for him who shall have borne the battle, and for his widow, and his orphan—to do all which may achieve and cherish a just, and a lasting peace, among ourselves, and with all nations.

[5] Psalms 19:9.

46

ABRAHAM LINCOLN

Last Public Address

April 11, 1865

On April 9, General Robert E. Lee surrendered to General Ulysses S. Grant at Appomattox Court House, Virginia. Lincoln prepared an address congratulating the Union armed forces and describing recon- struction. More than a year before, in December 1863, he had suggested a plan of reconstruction to Congress. Under his proposal, if a minority of adult white males in a state (10 percent of the number that had voted in 1860) took an oath pledging loyalty to the Constitution and obedience to wartime acts of the Union, including the Emancipation Proclamation, and then agreed to create a new state constitution prohibiting slavery, the state could reseat representatives and senators in the U.S. Congress. The Lincoln administration then began overseeing the reconstruction of Louisiana and other seceded states under these guidelines. Meanwhile, Congress proposed a reconstruction plan demanding a more arduous "ironclad" oath—the person taking it had to vow never to have supported the rebellion—and requiring a majority of adult white males to take the

From Roy P. Basler, ed., and Marion Dolores Pratt and Lloyd A. Dunlap, asst. eds., *The Collected Works of Abraham Lincoln* (New Brunswick, N.J.: Rutgers University Press, 1953–1955), 8:402–5.

oath before Congress would seat representatives and senators from the state. Lincoln pocket vetoed the bill, known as the Wade-Davis bill for the two members of Congress, Senator Benjamin F. Wade and Congressman Henry Winter Davis, who had sponsored it. By April 11, 1865, when Lincoln gave his address, Congress had yet to pass another reconstruction bill, although it had adopted the resolution for the antislavery constitutional amendment. Congress also had passed a bill creating the Freedmen's Bureau to help African Americans secure work, land, and equal rights. Lincoln signed the Freedmen's Bureau bill and also thought that some African Americans deserved the vote. He had privately made this suggestion to the provisional governor of Louisiana in March 1864, and he now made his view public. No one, of course, suspected that this speech would be Lincoln's last, except perhaps John Wilkes Booth, who assassinated Lincoln three days later.

The new constitution of Louisiana, declaring emancipation for the whole State, practically applies the Proclamation to the part previously excepted. . . .

We all agree that the seceded States, so called, are out of their proper practical relation with the Union; and that the sole object of the government, civil and military, in regard to those States is to again get them into that proper practical relation. I believe it is not only possible, but in fact, easier, to do this, without deciding, or even considering, whether these states have even been out of the Union, than with it. . . .

It is . . . unsatisfactory to some that the elective franchise [in Louisiana] is not given to the colored man. I would myself prefer that it were now conferred on the very intelligent, and on those who serve our cause as soldiers. . . .

Some twelve thousand voters in the heretofore slave-state of Louisiana have sworn allegiance to the Union, assumed to be the rightful political power of the State, held elections, organized a State government, adopted a free-state constitution, giving the benefit of public schools equally to black and white, and empowering the Legislature to confer the elective franchise upon the colored man. Their Legislature has already voted to ratify the constitutional amendment recently passed by Congress, abolishing slavery throughout the nation. . . . Now, if we reject, and spurn them, we do our utmost to disorganize and disperse them. We in effect say to the white men "You are worthless, or worse—we will neither help you, nor be helped by you." To the blacks we say "This cup of liberty which these, your old masters, hold to your lips, we will dash from you, and leave you to the chances of gathering the spilled and scattered contents in some vague and undefined when, where, and how." If this course, discouraging and paralyzing both white and black, has any tendency to bring Louisiana into proper practical relations with the Union, I have, so far, been unable to perceive it. If, on the contrary, we recognize, and sustain the new government of Louisiana the converse of all this is made true. We encourage the hearts, and nerve the arms of the twelve thousand to adhere to their work, and argue for it, and proselyte for it, and fight for it, and feed it, and grow it, and ripen it to a complete success. The colored man too, in seeing all united for him, is inspired with vigilance, and energy, and daring, to the same end. Grant that he desires the elective franchise, will he not attain it sooner by saving the already advanced steps toward it, than by running backward over them? . . . Again, if we reject Louisiana, we also reject one vote in favor of the proposed amendment to the national constitution. To meet this proposition, it has been argued that no more than three fourths of those States which have not attempted secession are necessary to validly ratify the amendment. I do not commit myself against this, further than to say that such a ratification would be questionable, and sure to be persistently questioned; while a ratification by three fourths of all the States would be unquestioned and unquestionable. . . .

What has been said of Louisiana will apply generally to other States. And yet so great peculiarities pertain to each state . . . that no exclusive, and inflexible plan can safely be prescribed as to details and colatterals. Such exclusive, and inflexible plan, would surely become a new entanglement. . . .

In the present "*situation*" as the phrase goes, it may be my duty to make some new announcement to the people of the South. I am considering, and shall not fail to act, when satisfied that action will be proper.

47

EDWARD D. TOWNSEND

Report on Meeting of African Americans with Union Officials

January 12, 1865

The low country of South Carolina and Georgia was the site of some of the most innovative reforms of wartime reconstruction. In the years since the Union had occupied the region in late 1861, African Americans and Union military and civilian officials had worked out various systems of land tenure for freed slaves and white Unionists in the area, but no single system prevailed. African American leaders and some of the more radical Republicans, such as Congressman Thaddeus Stevens of Pennsylvania, advocated large-scale confiscation of land from former rebels and redistribution of the land to freed people either for free or for a nominal fee. More conservative authorities preferred some sort of system of land rental, with the possibility of rent being paid in shares of crops (a system later formalized in the South and known as sharecropping).

Union general William Tecumseh Sherman, who had taken Atlanta in September 1864 and then proceeded on to his famous March to the Sea, entered the conversation in January 1865, not long after taking Savannah. Along with Secretary of War Edwin M. Stanton, who traveled to the region soon after Sherman arrived to help explore possible solutions, Sherman interviewed officials and residents about a variety of matters, from African American enlistment in the armed forces to labor arrangements to landholding. On January 12, Sherman and Stanton met with twenty African American men from the region, all of them ministers or church officials. The delegation, which included James Lynch, twenty-six-year-old "presiding elder" of the African Methodist Episcopal (AME) Church, chose Garrison Frazier, a sixty-seven-year-old Baptist minister, as its spokesman. Edward D. Townsend, an officer accompanying Stanton, prepared a report of the meeting, and Stanton gave a copy to Henry Ward Beecher, the brother of Harriet Beecher Stowe and the minister

From Edward D. Townsend, "Minutes of an Interview between the Colored Ministers and Church Officials at Savannah with the Secretary of War and Major-Gen. Sherman," January 12, 1865, in *New York Tribune*, February 13, 1865.

of Plymouth Church in New York City. Beecher read the transcript to his congregation on February 12, 1865, and gave it to the New York Tribune, *which published it the following day. Four days after Stanton and Sherman met with the delegation, Sherman issued Special Field Order 15, which confiscated roughly 400,000 acres of rebel land in the low country from South Carolina to Florida and distributed it to African Americans in forty-acre plots. The army also provided surplus mules and other pack animals to black families.*

Sherman's policy, which became known informally as "forty acres and a mule," was pioneering but not nearly as far-reaching as some of the plans of more radical reformers, who believed, rightly, that far more land would have to be redistributed, along with proper seeds and live-stock, to facilitate a smooth transition from slavery to freedom for African Americans in the South. Furthermore, legal title to the land distributed by Sherman was uncertain, which allowed President Andrew Johnson to return much of the land to its previous white owners in late 1865.

First: State what your understanding is in regard to the acts of Congress and President Lincoln's [Emancipation] proclamation, touching the condition of the colored people in the Rebel States.

Answer—So far as I understand President Lincoln's proclamation to the Rebellious States, it is, that if they would lay down their arms and submit to the laws of the United States before the first of January, 1863, all should be well; but if they did not, then all the slaves in the Rebel States should be free henceforth and forever. . . .

Second—State what you understand by Slavery and the freedom that was to be given by the President's proclamation.

Answer—Slavery is, receiving by *irresistible power* the work of another man, and not by his *consent*. The freedom, as I understand it, promised by the proclamation, is taking us from under the yoke of bondage, and placing us where we could reap the fruit of our own labor, take care of ourselves and assist the Government in maintaining our freedom.

Third: State in what manner you think you can take care of yourselves, and how can you best assist the Government in maintaining your freedom.

Answer. The way we can best take care of ourselves is to have land, and turn it and till it by our own labor—that is, by the labor of the women and children and old men; and we can soon maintain ourselves and have something to spare. . . . We want to be placed on land until we are able to buy it and make it our own.

Fourth: State in what manner you would rather live—whether scattered among the whites or in colonies by yourselves.

Answer: I would prefer to live by ourselves, for there is a prejudice against us in the South that will take years to get over; but I do not know that I can answer for my brethren. (Mr. Lynch says he thinks they should not be separated, but live together. All the other persons present, being questioned one by one, answer that they agree with Brother Frazier [that they should live separately].)

48

FREDERICK DOUGLASS

Speech in Memory of Abraham Lincoln
April 14, 1876

Like many Americans during and after the Civil War, Douglass frequently modified his views of Lincoln. In the early years of the war, Douglass regarded the president as too slow and conservative in supporting freedom and equal rights for all African Americans. But by the end of the war, Douglass was impressed with the progress that Lincoln had made in embracing emancipation and opening his mind to the possibility of equal citizenship for African Americans. Six weeks after Lincoln's assassination, in a speech on June 1, 1865, Douglass called him "emphatically the black man's president."[6]

By that time, Douglass had broken with William Lloyd Garrison and other abolitionists who contended that their work was done because slavery had been abolished. In fact, abolition was not secured until December 1865, when the Thirteenth Amendment was ratified. And for Douglass, freedom meant more than emancipation. It meant an end to discrimination and disfranchisement. Douglass pressed for voting rights for all adult African Americans, and he joined with those such as Elizabeth

[6] Michael Burlingame, "'Emphatically the Black Man's President': New Light on Frederick Douglass and Abraham Lincoln," *Lincoln Ledger* 4 (February 1996): 1, 3–5.

From *Oration by Frederick Douglass Delivered on the Occasion of the Unveiling of the Freedmen's Monument in Memory of Abraham Lincoln, in Lincoln Park, Washington, D.C. April 14th 1876* (Washington, D.C.: Gibson Brothers, 1876), 4–11, 14.

*Cady Stanton and Susan B. Anthony who demanded the vote and legal
equality for adult women of all races. In 1868, the Fourteenth Amendment was ratified, securing citizenship and "equal protection of the laws"
for African Americans. In 1870, the Fifteenth Amendment was adopted,
prohibiting states from denying the vote on the basis of color, although
they could still deny it on the basis of gender.*

*In the early 1870s, Douglass grew disillusioned with the federal
government. Especially troubling to him was the Republican Party's
retreat from the progressive policies of the early years of Reconstruction.
In the early 1870s, as the Republicans began to lose some of their power
in the federal and northern state governments, they lent less military and
financial support to Republican regimes in the South. By 1876, conservative southern whites had reestablished power in all but three of the
former Confederate states, and the administration of President Ulysses S.
Grant had backed off using the military to enforce black voting rights in
the South. Douglass's view of Lincoln darkened somewhat as he watched
Reconstruction unravel. He wished that the president had taken further
actions with a more lasting impact on behalf of African Americans.*

*On April 14, 1876, the anniversary of Lincoln's assassination,
Douglass gave voice to his modified view of Lincoln in his speech at the
dedication of the Freedmen's Memorial in Washington, D.C. (see Document 49). Douglass praised Lincoln as the "great liberator" but now
called him "pre-eminently the white man's President." Aside from the
speech by Douglass, the ceremony featured a reading of the Emancipation
Proclamation.*

We, the colored people, newly emancipated and rejoicing in our blood-
bought freedom, near the close of the first century in the life of this
Republic, have now and here unveiled, set apart, and dedicated a monument of enduring granite and bronze, in every line, feature, and figure
of which the men of this generation may read, and those of after-coming
generations may read, something of the exalted character and great
works of Abraham Lincoln, the first martyr President of the United
States. . . .

We claim for ourselves no superior devotion to the character, history,
and memory of the illustrious name whose monument we have here
dedicated to-day. We comprehend fully the relation of Abraham Lincoln
both to ourselves and to the white people of the United States. Truth is
proper and beautiful at all times and in all places, and it is never more
proper and beautiful in any case than when speaking of a great public

man whose example is likely to be commended for honor and imitation long after his departure to the solemn shades, the silent continents of eternity. It must be admitted, truth compels me to admit, even here in the presence of the monument we have erected to his memory, Abraham Lincoln was not, in the fullest sense of the word, either our man or our model. In his interests, in his associations, in his habits of thought, and in his prejudices, he was a white man.

He was pre-eminently the white man's President, entirely devoted to the welfare of white men. He was ready and willing at any time during the first years of his administration to deny, postpone, and sacrifice the rights of humanity in the colored people to promote the welfare of the white people of this country. In all his education and feeling he was an American of the Americans. He came into the Presidential chair upon one principle alone, namely, opposition to the extension of slavery. His arguments in furtherance of this policy had their motive and mainspring in his patriotic devotion to the interests of his own race. To protect, defend, and perpetuate slavery in the States where it existed Abraham Lincoln was not less ready than any other President to draw the sword of the nation. . . . He was willing to pursue, recapture, and send back the fugitive slave to his master, and to suppress a slave rising for liberty, though his guilty master were already in arms against the Government. The race to which we belong [was] not the special objects of his consideration. Knowing this, I concede to you, my white fellow-citizens, a pre-eminence in this worship at once full and supreme. First, midst, and last, you and yours were the objects of his deepest affection and his most earnest solicitude. You are the children of Abraham Lincoln. We are at best only his step-children; children by adoption, children by force of circumstances and necessity. To you it especially belongs to sound his praises, to preserve and perpetuate his memory, to multiply his statues, to hang his pictures high upon your walls, and commend his example, for to you he was a great and glorious friend and benefactor. . . . But while in the abundance of your wealth, and in the fulness of your just and patriotic devotion, you do all this, we entreat you to despise not the humble offering we this day unveil to view; for while Abraham Lincoln saved for you a country, he delivered us from a bondage, according to Jefferson, one hour of which was worse than ages of oppression your fathers rose in rebellion to oppose. . . .

. . . Though the Union was more to him than our freedom or our future, under his wise and beneficent rule we saw ourselves lifted from the depths of slavery to the heights of manhood; under his wise and beneficent rule, and by measures approved and vigorously pressed by him, we saw that the handwriting of ages, in the form of prejudice and prescription, was rapidly fading away from the face of our whole country. . . .

Can any colored man, or white man friendly to the freedom of all men, ever forget the night which followed the first day of January, 1863, when the world was to see if Abraham Lincoln would prove to be as good as his word? I shall never forget that memorable night, when in a distant city I waited and watched at a public meeting, with three thousand others not less anxious than myself, for the word of deliverance which we have heard read to-day. Nor shall I ever forget the outburst of joy and thanks-giving that rent the air when the lightning brought us the emancipation proclamation. In that happy hour we forgot all delay, and forgot all tardiness, forgot that the President had bribed the rebels to lay down their arms by a promise to withhold the bolt which would smite the slave-system with destruction; and we were thenceforward willing to allow the President all the latitude of time, phraseology, and every honorable device that statesmanship might require for the achievement of a great and beneficent measure of liberty and progress.

. . . I have said that President Lincoln was a white man, and shared the prejudices common to his countrymen towards the colored race. Looking back to his times and to the condition of his country, we are compelled to admit that this unfriendly feeling on his part may be safely set down as one element of his wonderful success in organizing the loyal American people for the tremendous conflict before them, and bringing them safely through that conflict. His great mission was to accomplish two things: first, to save his country from dismemberment and ruin; and, second, to free his country from the great crime of slavery. To do one or the other, or both, he must have the earnest sympathy and the powerful co-operation of his loyal fellow countrymen. Without this primary and essential condition to success his efforts must have been vain and utterly fruitless. Had he put the abolition of slavery before the salvation of the Union, he would have inevitably driven from him a powerful class of the American people and rendered resistance to rebellion impossible. Viewed from the genuine abolition ground, Mr. Lincoln seemed tardy, cold, dull, and indifferent; but measuring him by the sentiment of his country, a sentiment he was bound as a statesman to consult, he was swift, zealous, radical, and determined.

Though Mr. Lincoln shared the prejudices of his white fellow-countrymen against the negro, it is hardly necessary to say that in his heart of all hearts he loathed and hated slavery. The man who could say, "Fondly do we hope, fervently do we pray, that this mighty scourge of war shall soon pass away, yet if God wills it to continue till all wealth piled by two hundred years of bondage shall have been wasted, and each drop of blood drawn by the lash shall have been paid for by one drawn by the sword, the judgments of the Lord are true and righteous altogether," gives all the needed proof of his feeling on the subject of slavery. He was willing, while the South was loyal, that it should have its pound of flesh, because he thought that it was so nominated in the bond, but farther than this no earthly power could make him go. . . .

Fellow-citizens, the fourteenth day of April, 1865, of which this is the eleventh anniversary, is now and will ever remain a memorable day in the annals of this Republic. It was on the evening of this day, while a fierce and sanguinary rebellion was in the last stages of its desolating power; while its armies were broken and scattered before the invincible armies of Grant and Sherman; while a great nation, torn and rent by war, was already beginning to raise to the skies loud anthems of joy at the dawn of peace; it was startled, amazed, and overwhelmed by the crowing crime of slavery—the assassination of Abraham Lincoln. It was a new crime, a pure act of malice. It was the simple gratification of a hell-black spirit of revenge. But it has done good after all. It has filled the country with a deeper abhorrence of slavery and a deeper love for the great liberator.

49

THOMAS BALL

Freedmen's Memorial to Abraham Lincoln

1876

Also known as the Emancipation Memorial, this statue by Thomas Ball is located in the Capitol Hill area of Washington, D.C., in what is now called Lincoln Park. The drive to create the memorial began immediately after Lincoln's assassination on April 14, 1865. The planning began in 1866, and Ball completed the statue in 1876. Lincoln holds the Emancipation Proclamation in his right hand while a slave in chains kneels before him. The plaque on the memorial declares that funding to build the monument came entirely from the contributions of "emancipated citizens" who had been "declared free" by Lincoln's proclamation. At the dedication ceremony on April 14, 1876, the anniversary of Lincoln's assassination, the Emancipation Proclamation was read, and Frederick Douglass delivered an address (see Document 48).

Thomas Ball, *Freedmen's Memorial to Abraham Lincoln*, postcard (photographer unknown), ca. 1876.

50

HENRY W. HERRICK

Reading the Emancipation Proclamation in the Slaves' Cabin

1864

Henry W. Herrick was a New Hampshire artist who imagined this scene of an African American soldier reading a newspaper transcript of the Emancipation Proclamation aloud in a slave cabin somewhere in the South. Also known as The Midnight Hour, *the painting is most likely set on the night of January 1, 1863, when African Americans awaited the news of whether Abraham Lincoln had signed the final Proclamation as he had promised. On the floor is a stalk of sugarcane, which Herrick may purposely have painted to look like a whip.*

Henry W. Herrick, *Reading the Emancipation Proclamation in the Slaves' Cabin*, engraved by J. W. Watte (Hartford, Conn.: S. A. Peters, 1864).

READING THE
EMANCIPATION PROCLAMATION.

7

Historians Assess Emancipation

From the moment historians began writing about the Emancipation Proclamation, they have disagreed about its significance and legacy. Sometimes the disagreement is about Lincoln and his racial views. Sometimes it is about the relative merits of understanding emancipation from the perspective of politicians or of the slaves themselves. Always the debate has been shaped as much by contemporary issues as by the personal views of the authors. The essays that follow were written by two of the best-known historians of emancipation and the Civil War, James M. McPherson (Document 51) and Ira Berlin (Document 52).

51

JAMES M. McPHERSON

Who Freed the Slaves?

1996

James McPherson, a longtime professor of history at Princeton University, is the author of Battle Cry of Freedom: The Civil War Era, *a Pulitzer Prize–winning history of the Civil War, as well as more than ten other books, including* For Cause and Comrades: Why Men Fought in the Civil War *and* Tried by War: Abraham Lincoln as Commander-in-Chief, *both of which won the prestigious Lincoln Prize, awarded annually to the best book on the Civil War era. McPherson's earliest books, published in*

From James McPherson, "Who Freed the Slaves?" in *Drawn with the Sword: Reflections on the American Civil War*, ed. James M. McPherson (New York: Oxford University Press, 1996), 192–94, 196–207.

*the 1960s, examined abolitionists of the Civil War era. He returned to
this subject in his 1996 essay "Who Freed the Slaves?" assessing Lincoln's
role in emancipation in light of scholarship of the previous three decades.*

If we were to go out on the streets of almost any town in America and
ask the question posed by the title of this essay, probably nine out of ten
respondents would answer unhesitatingly, "Abraham Lincoln." Most of
them would cite the Emancipation Proclamation as the key document.
Some of the more reflective and better informed respondents would add
the Thirteenth Amendment and point to Lincoln's important role in its
adoption. And a few might qualify their answer by noting that without
Union military victory the Emancipation Proclamation and Thirteenth
Amendment would never have gone into effect, or at least would not
have applied to the states where most of the slaves lived. But, of course,
Lincoln was commander in chief of Union armies, so the credit for their
victories would belong mainly to him. The answer would still be the
same: Lincoln freed the slaves.

In recent years, though, this answer has been challenged as another
example of elitist history, of focusing only on the actions of great white
males and ignoring the actions of the overwhelming majority of the
people, who also make history. If we were to ask our question of profes-
sional historians, the reply would be quite different. For one thing, it
would not be simple or clear-cut. Many of them would answer along the
lines of "On the one hand . . . but on the other. . . ." They would speak
of ambivalence, ambiguity, nuances, paradox, irony. They would point
to Lincoln's gradualism, his slow and apparently reluctant decision for
emancipation, his revocation of emancipation orders by Generals John C.
Frémont and David Hunter, his exemption of border states and parts of
the Confederacy from the Emancipation Proclamation, his statements
seemingly endorsing white supremacy. They would say that the whole
issue is more complex than it appears—in other words many historians,
as is their wont, would not give a straight answer to the question.

But of those who did, a growing number would reply, as did a historian speaking to the Civil War Institute at Gettysburg College in 1991:
"THE SLAVES FREED THEMSELVES."[1] They saw the Civil War as a potential war for abolition well before Lincoln did. By flooding into Union
military camps in the South, they forced the issue of emancipation on

[1] Robert F. Engs, "The Great American Slave Rebellion," lecture delivered to the Civil
War Institute at Gettysburg College, June 27, 1991, p. 3 [McPherson note].

the Lincoln administration. By creating a situation in which Northern officials would either have to return them to slavery or acknowledge their freedom, these "contrabands," as they came to be called, "acted resolutely to place their freedom—and that of their posterity—on the wartime agenda." Union officers, then Congress, and finally Lincoln decided to confiscate this human property belonging to the enemy and put it to work for the Union in the form of servants, teamsters, laborers, and eventually soldiers in Northern armies. Weighed in the scale of war, these 190,000 black soldiers and sailors (and probably a larger number of black army laborers) tipped the balance in favor of Union victory. Even deep in the Confederate interior remote from the fighting fronts, with the departure of masters and overseers to the army, "leaving women and old men in charge, the balance of power gradually shifted in favor of slaves, undermining slavery on farms and plantations far from the line of battle."[2]

One of the leading exponents of the black self-emancipation thesis is the historian and theologian Vincent Harding, whose book *There Is a River: The Black Struggle for Freedom in America* has become almost a Bible for the argument. "While Lincoln continued to hesitate about the legal, constitutional, moral, and military aspects of the matter," Harding writes, "the relentless movement of the self-liberated fugitives into the Union lines" soon "approached and surpassed every level of force previously known. . . . Making themselves an unavoidable military and political issue . . . this overwhelming human movement . . . of self-freed men and women . . . took their freedom into their own hands." The Emancipation Proclamation, when it finally and belatedly came, merely "confirmed and gave ambiguous legal standing to the freedom which black people had already claimed through their own surging, living proclamations."[3]

During the 1980s this self-emancipation theme achieved the status of orthodoxy among social historians. The largest scholarly enterprise on the history of emancipation and the transition from a slave to a free society during the Civil War era, the Freedmen and Southern Society project at the University of Maryland, stamped its imprimatur on the

---

[2] Ira Berlin, Barbara J. Fields, Thavolia Glymph, Joseph P. Reidy, and Leslie S. Rowland, eds., *Freedom: A Documentary History of Emancipation 1861–1867*, Ser. I, Vol. I, *The Destruction of Slavery* (Cambridge, 1985), pp. 2, 10 [McPherson note].

[3] Vincent Harding, *There Is a River: The Black Struggle for Freedom in America* (New York, 1981), pp. 231, 230, 225, 226, 228, 235 [McPherson note].

interpretation. The slaves, wrote the editors of this project, were "the prime movers in securing their own liberty." . . .

How valid are these statements? First, we must recognize the considerable degree of truth in the main thesis. By coming into Union lines, by withdrawing their labor from Confederate owners, by working for the Union army and fighting as soldiers in it, slaves did play an active part in achieving their own freedom and, for that matter, in preserving the Union. Like workers, immigrants, women, and other nonelites, slaves were neither passive victims nor pawns of powerful white males who loom so large in our traditional image of American history. They too played a part in determining their own destiny; they too made a history that historians have finally discovered. That is all to the good. But by challenging the "myth" that Lincoln freed the slaves, proponents of the self-emancipation thesis are in danger of creating another myth—that he had little to do with it. It may turn out, upon close examination, that the traditional answer to the question "Who Freed the Slaves?" is closer to being the right answer than is the new and currently more fashionable answer.

First, one must ask what was the sine qua non of emancipation in the 1860s—the essential condition, the one thing without which it would not have happened. The clear answer is the war. Without the Civil War there would have been no confiscation act, no Emancipation Proclamation, no Thirteenth Amendment (not to mention the Fourteenth and Fifteenth), certainly no self-emancipation, and almost certainly no end of slavery for several more decades at least. Slavery had existed in North America for more than two centuries before 1861, but except for a tiny fraction of slaves who fought in the Revolution, or escaped, or bought their freedom, there had been no self-emancipation during that time. Every slave insurrection or insurrection conspiracy failed in the end. On the eve of the Civil War, plantation agriculture was more profitable, slavery more entrenched, slave owners more prosperous, and the "slave power" more dominant within the South if not in the nation at large than it had ever been. Without the war, the door to freedom would have remained closed for an indeterminate length of time.

What brought the war and opened that door? The answer, of course, is complex as well as controversial. A short and simplified summary is that secession and the refusal of the United States government to recognize the legitimacy of secession brought on the war. In both of these matters Abraham Lincoln moves to center stage. Seven states seceded and formed the Confederacy because he won election to the presidency on an antislavery platform; four more seceded after shooting broke out when he refused to evacuate Fort Sumter; the shooting escalated to full-scale war because he called out the troops to suppress rebellion. The common denominator in all of the steps that opened the door to freedom was the active agency of Abraham Lincoln as antislavery political leader, president-elect, president, and commander in chief. . . .

But, we must ask, would not the election of *any* Republican in 1860 have provoked secession? Probably not, if the candidate had been Edward Bates[4] — who might conceivably have won the election but had no chance of winning the nomination. Yes, almost certainly, if William H. Seward had been the nominee. Seward's earlier talk of a "higher law" and an "irrepressible conflict" had given him a more radical reputation than Lincoln. But Seward might not have won the election. More to the point, if he had won, seven states would undoubtedly have seceded but Seward would have favored compromises and concessions to keep others from going out and perhaps to lure those seven back in. Most important of all, he would have evacuated Fort Sumter and thereby extinguished the spark that threatened to flame into war.

As it was, Seward did his best to compel Lincoln into concessions and evacuation of the fort. But Lincoln stood firm. When Seward flirted with the notion of supporting the Crittenden Compromise,[5] which would have repudiated the Republican platform by permitting the expansion of slavery, Lincoln stiffened the backbones of Seward and other key Republican leaders. "Entertain no proposition for a compromise in regard to the *extension* of slavery," he wrote to them. "The tug has to come, & better now, than any time hereafter." Crittenden's compromise "would lose us everything we gained by the election." It "acknowledges

[4] Edward Bates was a Missouri attorney prominent first in the Whig and then the Republican Party. Lincoln appointed him attorney general. The Border State conservative helped offset cabinet members with a more radical reputation, such as William Henry Seward of New York.

[5] The Crittenden Compromise was a set of measures proposed by Senator John J. Crittenden of Kentucky in December 1860 to resolve the congressional conflict over slavery and to stem the tide of secession. At the heart of the proposal was the reestablishment of the old Missouri Compromise line, with slavery prohibited north of it and allowed south of it. But whereas the old line applied only to the Louisiana Purchase area, the new one would extend all the way to the Pacific Ocean. Because it might have allowed slavery to expand farther west than it already reached, the compromise violated the principle of the non-expansion of slavery that had been central to the platform of Abraham Lincoln, who was now president-elect. Congress tabled the compromise at the end of December. The Crittenden Compromise should not be confused with the Crittenden Resolution of July 1861, also proposed by Senator Crittenden, which pledged that the war would leave slavery untouched.

that slavery has equal rights with liberty, and surrenders all we have contended for. . . . We have just carried an election on principles fairly stated to the people. Now we are told in advance, the government shall be broken up, unless we surrender to those we have beaten. . . . If we surrender, it is the end of us. They will repeat the experiment upon us *ad libitum*. A year will not pass, till we shall have to take Cuba as a condition upon which they will stay in the Union."[6]

It is worth emphasizing here that the common denominator in these letters from Lincoln to Republican leaders was slavery. To be sure, on the matters of slavery where it already existed and enforcement of the fugitive slave provision of the Constitution, Lincoln was willing to reassure the South. But on the crucial issue of 1860, slavery in the territories, he refused to compromise, and this refusal kept his party in line. . . . As Lincoln expressed it in a private letter to his old friend Alexander Stephens, "You think slavery is *right* and ought to be extended; while we think it is *wrong* and ought to be restricted. That I suppose is the rub" [see Document 3].

It was indeed the rub. Even more than in his election to the presidency, Lincoln's refusal to compromise on the expansion of slavery or on Fort Sumter proved decisive. If another person had been in his place, the course of history—and of emancipation—would have been different. Here again we have without question a sine qua non.

It is quite true that once the war started, Lincoln moved more slowly and apparently more reluctantly toward making it a war for emancipation than black leaders, abolitionists, radical Republicans, and the slaves themselves wanted him to move. He did reassure Southern whites that he had no intention and no constitutional power to interfere with slavery in the states. In September 1861 and May 1862 he revoked orders by Generals Frémont and Hunter freeing the slaves of Confederates in their military districts. In December 1861 he forced Secretary of War Simon Cameron to delete from his annual report a paragraph recommending the freeing and arming of slaves. And though Lincoln signed the confiscation acts of August 1861 and July 1862 that freed some slaves owned by Confederates, this legislation did not come from his initiative. Out in the field it was the slaves who escaped to Union lines and officers like General Benjamin Butler who accepted them as "contraband of war" that took the initiative.

---

[6] Roy P. Basler ed., *The Collected Works of Abraham Lincoln*, 9 vols. (New Brunswick, N.J., 1953–1955), IV, 149–51, 154, 183, 155, 172 [McPherson note].

All of this appears to support the thesis that slaves emancipated themselves and that Lincoln's image as emancipator is a myth. But let us take a closer look. It seems clear today, as it did in 1861, that no matter how many thousands of slaves came into Union lines, the ultimate fate of the millions who did not, as well as the fate of the institution of slavery itself, depended on the outcome of the war. If the North won, slavery would be weakened if not destroyed; if the Confederacy won, slavery would survive and perhaps grow stronger from the postwar territorial expansion of an independent and confident slave power. Thus Lincoln's emphasis on the priority of Union had positive implications for emancipation, while precipitate or premature actions against slavery might jeopardize the cause of Union and therefore boomerang in favor of slavery.

Lincoln's chief concern in 1861 was to maintain a united coalition of War Democrats and border-state Unionists as well as Republicans in support of the war effort. To do this he considered it essential to define the war as being waged solely for Union, which united this coalition, and not a war against slavery, which would fragment it. When General Frémont issued his emancipation edict in Missouri on August 30, 1861, the political and military efforts to prevent Kentucky, Maryland, and Missouri from seceding and to cultivate Unionists in western Virginia and eastern Tennessee were at a crucial stage, balancing on a knife edge. To keep his fragile coalition from falling apart, therefore, Lincoln rescinded Frémont's order.

Almost certainly this was the right decision at the time. Lincoln's greatest skills as a political leader were his sensitivity to public opinion and his sense of timing. Within six months of his revocation of Frémont's order, he began moving toward a stronger antislavery position. During the spring and early summer of 1862 he alternately coaxed and prodded border-state Unionists toward recognition of the inevitable escalation of the conflict into a war against slavery and toward acceptance of his plan for compensated emancipation in their states. He warned them that the "friction and abrasion" of a war that had by this time swept every institution into its maelstrom could not leave slavery untouched. But the border states remained deaf to Lincoln's warnings and refused to consider his offer of federally compensated emancipation.

By July 1862, Lincoln turned a decisive corner toward abolition. He made up his mind to issue an emancipation proclamation. Whereas a year earlier, even three months earlier, Lincoln had believed that avoidance of such a drastic step was necessary to maintain that knife-edge balance in the Union coalition, things had now changed. The escalation of the war in scope and fury had mobilized all the resources of both sides, including the slave labor force of the Confederacy. . . . The risks of alienating the border states and Northern Democrats, Lincoln now believed, were outweighed by the opportunity to energize the Republican majority and to mobilize part of the slave population for the cause of Union—and freedom. When Lincoln told his cabinet on July 22, 1862, that he had decided to issue an emancipation proclamation, [Postmaster General] Montgomery Blair, speaking for the forces of conservatism in the North and border states, warned of the consequences among these groups if he did so. But Lincoln was done conciliating them. He had tried to make the border states see reason; now "we must make the forward movement" without them. "They [will] acquiesce, if not immediately, soon." As for the Northern Democrats, "their clubs would be used against us take what course we might."[7]

Two years later, speaking to a visiting delegation of abolitionists, Lincoln explained why he had moved more slowly against slavery than they had urged. Having taken an oath to preserve and defend the Constitution, which protected slavery, "I did not consider that I had a *right* to touch the 'State' institution of 'Slavery' until all other measures for restoring the Union had failed. . . . The moment came when I felt that slavery must die that the nation might live! . . . Many of my strongest supporters urged *Emancipation* before I thought it indispensable, and, I may say, before I thought the country ready for it. It is my conviction that, had the proclamation been issued even six months earlier than it was, public sentiment would not have sustained it."[8]

Lincoln actually could have made a case that the country had not been ready for the Emancipation Proclamation in September 1862, even in January 1863. Democratic gains in the Northern congressional elections of 1862 resulted in part from a voter backlash against the preliminary Emancipation Proclamation. The morale crisis in Union armies and swelling Copperhead strength during the winter of 1863 grew in part from a resentful conviction that Lincoln had unconstitutionally transformed the purpose of the war from restoring the Union to freeing the slaves. Without question, this issue bitterly divided the Northern people and threatened fatally to erode support for the war effort—the very consequence Lincoln had feared in 1861 and Montgomery Blair had warned against in 1862. Not until after the twin military victories at Gettysburg

[7] John G. Nicolay and John Hay, *Abraham Lincoln: A History*, 10 vols. (New York, 1890), VI, 158–63 [McPherson note].

[8] Francis B. Carpenter, *Six Months at the White House with Abraham Lincoln* (New York, 1866), pp. 76–77 [McPherson note].

and Vicksburg[9] did this divisiveness diminish and emancipation gain a clear mandate in the off-year elections of 1863. In his annual message of December 1863, Lincoln conceded that the Emancipation Proclamation a year earlier had been "followed by dark and doubtful days." But now, he added, "the crisis which threatened to divide the friends of the Union is past."[10]

Even that statement turned out to be premature and overoptimistic. In the summer of 1864, Northern morale again plummeted and the emancipation issue once more threatened to undermine the war effort. By August, Grant's campaign in Virginia had bogged down in the trenches after enormous casualties. Sherman seemed similarly thwarted before Atlanta and smaller Union armies elsewhere appeared to be accomplishing nothing. War weariness and defeatism corroded the will of Northerners as they contemplated the staggering cost of this conflict in the lives of their young men. Lincoln came under enormous pressure to open peace negotiations to end the slaughter. Even though Jefferson Davis insisted that Confederate independence was his essential condition for peace, Northern Democrats managed to convince many Northern people that only Lincoln's insistence on emancipation blocked peace. A typical Democratic newspaper editorial declared that "tens of thousands of white men must yet bite the dust to allay the negro mania of the President."[11]

Even Republicans like Horace Greeley, who had criticized Lincoln two years earlier for slowness to embrace emancipation, now criticized him for refusing to abandon it as a precondition for negotiations. The Democratic national convention adopted a platform for the 1864 presidential election calling for peace negotiations to restore the Union with slavery. Every political observer, including Lincoln himself, believed in August that the Republicans would lose the election. The *New York Times* editor and Republican national chairman Henry Raymond told Lincoln that "two special causes are assigned [for] this great reaction in public sentiment, — the want of military success, and the impression . . . that we *can* have peace with Union if we would. . . [but that you are] fighting not for Union but for the abolition of slavery.[12]

---

[9] On July 4, 1863, the day after the Union victory at Gettysburg, the Confederate garrison at Vicksburg, Mississippi, a strategic point on the Mississippi River, surrendered to the Union general Ulysses S. Grant.

[10] Basler, ed., *Collected Works of Lincoln*, VII, 49–50 [McPherson note].

[11] *Columbus Crisis*, Aug. 3, 1864 [McPherson note].

[12] Raymond to Lincoln, Aug. 22, 1864, in Basler, ed., *Collected Works of Lincoln*, VII, 518 [McPherson note].

The pressure on Lincoln to back down on emancipation caused him to waver temporarily but not to buckle. Instead, he told weak-kneed Republicans that "no human power can subdue this rebellion without using the Emancipation lever as I have done." More than one hundred thousand black soldiers and sailors were fighting for the Union, said Lincoln. They would not do so if they thought the North intended to "betray them. . . . If they stake their lives for us they must be prompted by the strongest motive . . . the promise of freedom. And the promise being made, must be kept. . . . There have been men who proposed to me to return to slavery the black warriors" who had fought for the Union. "I should be damned in time & in eternity for so doing. The world shall know that I will keep my faith to friends and enemies, come what will."[13]

When Lincoln said this, he fully expected to lose the election. In effect, he was saying that he would rather be right than president. In many ways this was his finest hour. As matters turned out, of course, he was both right and president. Sherman's capture of Atlanta, [General Philip] Sheridan's victories in the Shenandoah Valley, and military success elsewhere transformed the Northern mood from deepest despair in August 1864 to determined confidence by November, and Lincoln was triumphantly reelected. He won without compromising one inch on the emancipation question.

It is instructive to consider two possible alternatives to this outcome. If the Democrats had won, at best the Union would have been restored without a Thirteenth Amendment; at worst the Confederacy would have achieved its independence. In either case the institution of slavery would have survived. That this did not happen was owing more to the steadfast purpose of Abraham Lincoln than to any other single factor.

The proponents of the self-emancipation thesis, however, would avow that all of this is irrelevant. . . . But I disagree. The tide of freedom could have been swept back. On numerous occasions during the war, it was. . . . The editors of the Freedmen's and Southern Society project, the most scholarly advocates of the self-emancipation thesis, acknowledge that "Southern armies could recapture black people who had already reached Union lines. . . . Indeed, any Union retreat could reverse the process of liberation and throw men and women who had tasted freedom back into

---

[13] Lincoln to Charles D. Robinson, Aug. 17, 1864; interview of Lincoln with Alexander W. Randall and Joseph T. Mills, Aug. 19, 1864, both in ibid., 500, 506–7 [McPherson note].

bondage. . . . Their travail testified to the link between the military success of the Northern armies and the liberty of Southern slaves."[14]

Precisely. That is the crucial point. Slaves did not emancipate themselves; they were liberated by Union armies. Freedom quite literally
came from the barrel of a gun. And who was the commander in chief
that called these armies into being, appointed their generals, and gave
them direction and purpose? There, indubitably, is our sine qua non.

But let us grant that once the war was carried into slave territory,
no matter how it came out the ensuing "friction and abrasion" would
have enabled thousands of slaves to escape to freedom. In that respect,
a degree of self-emancipation did occur. But even on a large scale, such
emancipation was very different from *the abolition of the institution of
slavery*. During the American Revolution almost as large a percentage
of the slaves won freedom by coming within British lines as achieved
liberation by coming within Union lines during the Civil War. Yet slavery survived the Revolution. Ending the institution of bondage required
Union victory; it required Lincoln's reelection in 1864; it required the
Thirteenth Amendment. Lincoln played a vital role, indeed the central
role, in all of these achievements. It was also his policies and his skillful political leadership that set in motion the processes by which the
reconstructed or Unionist states of Louisiana, Arkansas, Tennessee,
Maryland, and Missouri abolished the institution in those states during
the war itself.

Regrettably, Lincoln did not live to see the final ratification of the
Thirteenth Amendment. But if he had never lived, it seems safe to say
that we would not have had a Thirteenth Amendment in 1865. In that
sense, the traditional answer to the question "Who Freed the Slaves?" is
the right answer. Lincoln did not accomplish this in the manner sometimes symbolically portrayed, breaking the chains of helpless and passive bondsmen with the stroke of a pen by signing the Emancipation
Proclamation. But by pronouncing slavery a moral evil that must come
to an end and then winning the presidency in 1860, provoking the South
to secede, by refusing to compromise on the issue of slavery's expansion or on Fort Sumter, by careful leadership and timing that kept a
fragile Unionist coalition together in the first year of war and committed
it to emancipation in the second, by refusing to compromise this policy
once he had adopted it, and by prosecuting the war to unconditional victory as commander in chief of an army of liberation, Abraham Lincoln
freed the slaves.

[14]Berlin et al., eds., *The Destruction of Slavery*, pp. 35–36 [McPherson note].

52

IRA BERLIN

Who Freed the Slaves? Emancipation and Its Meaning

1997

A professor at the University of Maryland, Ira Berlin has written a number of influential books on American slavery, including Many Thousands Gone: The First Two Centuries of Slavery in North America *and* Generations of Captivity: A History of African-American Slaves, *both of which won multiple prizes. Until 1991, Berlin was the director of the Freedmen and Southern Society project, which has published numerous volumes on African Americans' experience of emancipation during the Civil War and Reconstruction. One of those volumes,* Free at Last, *won the Lincoln Prize in 1994. Berlin's work on the project provided him with a rich understanding of the meaning of emancipation for African Americans, and he reflected on this meaning in his essay "Who Freed the Slaves?" which offered a response to James M. McPherson's essay of the same name (Document 51).*

The debate over the origins of Civil War emancipation in the American South can be parsed in such a way as to divide historians into two camps: those who understand emancipation primarily as the product of the slaves' struggle to free themselves, and those who see the Great Emancipator's hand at work. James McPherson made precisely such a division. While acknowledging the role of the slaves in their own liberation, he came down heavily on the side of Lincoln's authorship of emancipation, a fact he maintained most ordinary Americans grasped intuitively but one that eluded some scholars whose taste for the complex, the nuanced, and the ironic had blinded them to the obvious. McPherson characterized the critics of Lincoln's preeminence—advocates of what he called the "self-emancipation thesis"—as scholarly populists

---

Ira Berlin, "Who Freed the Slaves? Emancipation and Its Meaning," in *Union and Emancipation: Essays on Politics and Race in the Civil War Era*, ed. David W. Blight and Brooks D. Simpson (Kent, Ohio: Kent State University Press, 1997), 107–21.

whose stock in trade was a celebration of the "so-called 'non-elite.'"
Such scholars, McPherson implied, denied the historical role of "white
males," and perhaps all regularly constituted authority, in a misguided
celebration of the masses.

McPherson singled out Vincent Harding as the high priest of the
self-emancipationists, declaring Harding's *There Is a River: The Black
Struggle for Freedom in America* "almost a Bible" for the revisionists.[15]
But there were other culprits, among them Robert F. Engs and myself
and my colleagues on the Freedmen and Southern Society Project at
the University of Maryland, whose multivolume documentary history,
Freedom, he termed "the largest scholarly enterprise on the history of
emancipation."[16] He gave special attention to Barbara Jeanne Fields, a
member of the project who had articulated many of *Freedom*'s themes
on Ken Burns's TV documentary "The Civil War."[17] Together, these
historians were responsible for elevating the "self-emancipation thesis"
into what McPherson called "a new orthodoxy." . . .

Lincoln's proclamation of January 1, 1863, as its critics have noted,
freed not a single slave who was not already entitled to freedom under
legislation passed by Congress the previous year. It applied only to the
slaves in territories then beyond the reach of Federal authority. It specifically exempted Tennessee and Union-occupied portions of Louisiana
and Virginia, and it left slavery in the loyal border states—Delaware,
Maryland, Kentucky, and Missouri—untouched. Indeed, in a strict

[15] Vincent Harding, *There Is a River: The Black Struggle for Freedom in America* (New
York: Harcourt, Brace, Jovanovich, 1981) [Berlin note].

[16] Since most historical scholarship is carried on in the solitary artisan tradition, it is
easy to exaggerate the numbers involved in collaborative historical research. Sad to say,
"the largest scholarly enterprise on the history of emancipation" bears little resemblance
to the Manhattan Project or major research projects in the social sciences. Since its
inception in 1976, fewer than a dozen historians have been associated with the project—
never more than five at any one time. Besides myself, the editors of the four volumes in
print are Barbara Jeanne Fields, Thavolia Glymph, Steven Miller, Joseph P. Reidy, Leslie
S. Rowland, and Julie Saville.

The project's main work has been published by Cambridge Univ. Press under the
title *Freedom: A Documentary History of Emancipation*. Thus far four volumes are in
print: *The Destruction of Slavery* (1985); *The Wartime Genesis of Free Labor: The Upper
South* (1993); *The Wartime Genesis of Free Labor: The Lower South* (1991); and *The Black
Military Experience* (1982). In 1992, the New Press published an abridgment of the first
four volumes entitled *Free at Last: A Documentary History of Slavery, Freedom, and the
Civil War*, and Cambridge has issued a volume entitled *Slaves No More* [Berlin note].

[17] Barbara Jeanne Fields, "Who Freed the Slaves?" in *The Civil War: An Illustrated
History*, ed. Geoffrey C. Ward with Ken Burns and Ric Burns (New York: Knopf, 1990);
178–81. One particularly unfortunate aspect of the debate is the tendency to divide the
participants along racial lines and to identify black scholars as the proponents of the
slave's agency. See James M. McPherson, "Liberating Lincoln," *New York Review of
Books*, Apr. 21, 1994 [Berlin note].

sense, the Proclamation went no further than the Second Confiscation Act of July 1862, which freed all slaves who entered Union lines professing that their owners were disloyal, as well as those slaves who fell under Federal control as Union troops occupied Confederate territory. Moreover, at its fullest, the Emancipation Proclamation rested upon the President's wartime power as commander in chief and was subject to constitutional challenge. Lincoln recognized the limitations of his ill-defined wartime authority, and, as his commitment to emancipation grew firmer in 1863 and 1864, he pressed for passage of a constitutional amendment to affirm slavery's destruction.

What then was the point of the Proclamation? It spoke in muffled tones that heralded not the dawn of universal liberty but the compromised and piecemeal arrival of an undefined freedom. Indeed, the Proclamation's flat prose, ridiculed by the late Richard Hofstadter as having "all the moral grandeur of a bill of lading," suggests that the true authorship of African American freedom lies elsewhere—not at the top of American society but at its base.[18] McPherson . . . and others are correct in noting that the editors of the Freedmen and Southern Society Project and other revisionists built upon this insight.

From the first guns at Fort Sumter, the strongest advocates of emancipation were the slaves themselves. Lacking political standing or a public voice, forbidden access to the weapons of war, slaves nevertheless tossed aside the grand pronouncements of Lincoln and other Union leaders that the sectional conflict was only a war for national unity. Instead, they moved directly to put their own freedom—and that of their posterity—atop the national agenda. Steadily, as opportunities arose, slaves risked their all for freedom. By abandoning their owners, coming uninvited into Union lines, and offering their lives and labor in the Federal cause, slaves forced Federal soldiers at the lowest level to recognize their importance to the Union's success. That understanding traveled quickly up the chain of command. In time, it became evident to even the most obtuse Federal commanders that every slave who crossed into Union lines was a double gain: one subtracted from the Confederacy and one added to the Union. The slaves' resolute determination to secure their liberty converted many white Northern Americans—soldiers and civilians alike—to the view that the security of the Union depended upon the destruction of slavery. Eventually, this belief tipped the balance in

[18] Richard Hofstadter, *The American Political Tradition and the Men Who Made It* (New York: Vintage, 1948), 132. [Berlin note].

favor of freedom, even among Yankees who displayed little interest in the question of slavery and no affection for black people.

Slaves were not without allies. Abolitionists, black and white, dismissed the Republican doctrine that slavery should be respected and given constitutional protection where it existed. Instead, abolitionists, like the slaves, saw the war as an opportunity to assault a system they believed was immoral and pressed for its extradition. Rather than condemn slavery from the comfort of their drawing rooms, some radical opponents of slavery volunteered to fight slavery on its own terrain, strapped on their haversacks, and marched south as part of the Union army. But soldiering was young men's work, and sex, age, condition, and circumstance barred many radicals from the Federal army. Most abolitionists could only fume against slavery in petitions, editorials, and sermons. Although their campaign on behalf of emancipation laid the foundation for congressional and then presidential action against slavery, the majority of abolitionists had but slender means to attack slavery directly. Only slaves had both the commitment and the opportunity to initiate the assault on slavery.

Some slaves did not even wait for the war to begin. In March 1861, before the first shots at Fort Sumter, eight runaways presented themselves at Fort Pickens, a federal installation in Florida, "entertaining the idea"—in the words of the fort's commanded—that Federal forces "were placed here to protect them and grant them their freedom." The commander believed otherwise and delivered the slaves to the local sheriff, who returned them to their owner.[19] Although their mission failed, these eight runaways were only the first to evince publicly a conviction that eventually became widespread throughout the slave community.

In making the connection between the war and freedom, slaves also understood that a Union victory was imperative. They did what they could to secure it, throwing their full weight behind the Federal cause, volunteering their services as teamsters, stable hands, and boatmen; butchers, bakers, and cooks; nurses, orderlies, and laundresses; blacksmiths, coopers, and carpenters; and, by the tens of thousands, as common laborers. Slaves "tabooed" those few in their ranks who shunned the effort.[20] Hundreds of thousands of black men and women would

[19] U.S. War Department, *The War of the Rebellion: A Compilation of the Official Records of the Union and Confederate Armies*, 128 vols. (Washington, D.C.: GPO, 1880–1901), ser. 2, vol. 1, 750 (hereafter cited as *OR*)... [Berlin note].

[20] *Freedom: A Documentary History of Emancipation, 1861–1867*, ser. 1, vol. 2, *The Wartime Genesis of Free Labor: The Upper South*, ed. Ira Berlin, Steven F. Miller, Joseph P. Reidy, and Leslie S. Rowland (Cambridge: Cambridge University Press, 1993), 123–26 [Berlin note].

work for the Union army, and more than 135,000 slave men became Union soldiers. Even deep within the Confederacy, where escape to Federal lines was impossible, slaves did what they could to undermine the Confederacy and strengthen the Union—from aiding escaped Northern prisoners of war to praying for Northern military success. With their loyalty, their labor, and their lives, slaves provided crucial muscle and blood in support of the Federal war effort. No one was more responsible for smashing the shackles of slavery than the slaves.

Still, slaves could not free themselves. Nowhere in the four volumes of *Freedom* do the editors of the Freedmen and Southern Society Project claim they did. Nowhere in the four volumes of *Freedom* is the term *self-emancipation* employed.... Slaves could—and they did—put the issue of freedom on the wartime agenda; they could—and they did—make certain that the question of their liberation did not disappear in the complex welter of the war; they could—and they did—ensure that there was no retreat from the commitment to emancipation once the issue was drawn. In short, they did what was in their power to do with the weapons they had. They could not vote, pass laws, issue field orders, or promulgate great proclamations. That was the realm of citizens, legislators, military officers, and the president. However, the actions of the slaves made it possible and necessary for citizens, legislators, military officers, and the president to act. Slaves were the prime movers in the emancipation drama, not the sole movers. Slaves set others in motion, including many who would never have moved if left to their own devices. How they did so is nothing less than the story of emancipation.[21]

Among the slaves' first students were Union soldiers of the lowest rank. Arriving in the South with little direct knowledge of slavery and often contemptuous of black people, Federal soldiers encountered slaves who were eager to test their owners' fulminations against Yankee abolitionists and black Republicans. Union soldiers soon found their camps inundated with slaves, often breathless, tattered, and bearing marks of abuse who were seeking sanctuary and offering to assist them in any way possible. In so doing, slaves took a considerable risk. They not only faced sure punishment if captured, but Union soldiers often turned upon them violently.

Still, some gained entry into Federal lines, where they found work aplenty. Sometimes the slaves' labor cut to the heart of the soldiers' military mission, as slaves understood that the enemy of their enemy was their friend and were pleased to impart information about Confederate

[21] The argument is fully explicated in *The Destruction of Slavery* [Berlin note].

troop movements, assist in the construction of Federal fortifications, and guide Union troops through a strange countryside. But just as often, slaves ingratiated themselves with Federal troops in ways that had no particular military significance. They foraged for firewood, cooked food, cleaned camps, and did dozens of onerous jobs that otherwise would have fallen to the soldiers themselves.

Northern soldiers did not have to be Free-Soilers, abolitionists, or even radical egalitarians to appreciate these valuable services. Thus, soldiers were dismayed to discover that they had violated orders by harboring the fugitives. They were more upset when the men and women who cleaned their camps and cooked their food were dragged off to certain punishment by angry masters or mistresses. Indeed, even those soldiers who stoutly maintained that they fought only for Union bitterly resented being implicated in the punishment of men and women who had done nothing more than do them a good turn in exchange for a blanket and a few morsels of food. "I don't care a damn for the darkies," declared one midwestern volunteer in March 1862, "but I couldn't help to send a runaway nigger back. I'm blamed if I could."[22] The "blame" many Union soldiers felt at being implicated in slavery was compounded by their outrage when they discovered that the very same men and women they had returned to bondage were being mobilized by the Confederate enemy against them. To Union soldiers, the folly of denying themselves the resources that their enemy used freely—indeed, assisting their enemy in maintaining those resources—seemed senseless to the point of absurdity. . . .

Faced with conflicting demands—the need for labor versus the requirements of Federal policy; the desire to protect hapless fugitives versus the demands of Unionist owners—many Union soldiers and officers searched for ways to stand clear of the entire business, to be, in the idiom of the day, neither slave catcher nor slave stealer. Union policy toward slaves beginning in the fall of 1861 through the spring of 1862 was designed to eliminate the "devilish nigger question," as one Maryland official called it, by excluding fugitive slaves from Union lines. But slaves refused to surrender their belief that the Federal army was a refuge from slavery; they would not allow Federal soldiers to evade the central reality of the war.

Slaves continued to press themselves on soldiers, bringing gifts of food, information, and of course labor. There always seemed to be a few

---

[22] Quoted in James M. McPherson, *What They Fought For, 1861–1865* (Baton Rouge: Louisiana State Univ. Press, 1994), 59 [Berlin note].

Yankee soldiers who, for whatever reason, sheltered runaways, and a handful who encouraged slave flight. But even when the fugitives were denied entry to Federal lines, they camped outside, just far enough away to avoid expulsion by Union commanders, just close enough to avoid capture by Confederate soldiers. Meanwhile, alert for ways to turn the military conflict to their own advantage, slaves continued to search the seams of Federal policy looking for an opening: the ascent of a sympathetic commander or a crisis that might inflate the value of their knowledge or their muscle. Many learned the letter of the law so that they could seemingly recite from memory passages from the House Resolution of 1861, the additional Article of War of March 1862, the First Confiscation Act of August 1861, or the Second Confiscation Act of July 1862.[23] Time and time again, slaves forced Federal soldiers and officers to make the choice, a choice that became easier as the Union army's need for labor grew. Change did not come at once, but it came.

The lessons slaves taught soldiers and soldiers taught officers slowly ascended the Union chain of command and in November 1861 reached Lincoln's cabinet for the first time. Secretary of War Simon Cameron publicly endorsed a proposal to arm slaves to fight for the Union and freedom.[24] Lincoln quieted Cameron and packed him off to Russia as minister, but the slaves continued undeterred to press their case.

The slow shift in Federal policy gained momentum as the Union army penetrated deeper into the Confederacy, where slaveholders were not reluctant Unionists but outright rebels. In these circumstances, some field commanders became quick learners. Their respect for the old order yielded to a willingness to challenge the rights of the master and finally to a firm determination to extirpate slavery. Others learned slowly, imperfectly, or not at all. However, before long, the most obdurate generals began to disappear from places of high command, and the quick studies rose to the top.

The broad outline of the story was always the same. Slaves forced the issue: what should be done with them? Deciding the matter was always difficult, for it required a choice between the contradictory interests of

[23]The House Resolution of 1861, also known as the Crittenden Resolution, declared that the war was not being fought to overthrow or interfere with "the rights of established institutions" of the seceded states, by which Congress meant slavery. The additional Article of War of March 1862 was part of the Militia Act, passed by Congress on March 13, 1862. It prohibited Union military officials from returning slaves to owners in rebellion.

[24]Edward McPherson, *The Political History of the United States of America during the Great Rebellion, 1860–1865,* 2d ed. (Washington, D.C.: Philip & Solomons, 1865), 249, 416 [Berlin note].

the master and of the slave. At first slaveholders held the upper hand, but in time the advantage slipped to the slaves. When the slaves' loyalty became more valuable than the masters' in the eyes of Federal authorities, the Federal army became the slaves' willing partner rather than its reluctant enemy. The process by which the Union army became an army of liberation was in its essence political and reveals how black people had been incorporated into American politics long before they had the vote, the right to petition, or independent standing at law. . . .

The lesson that slaves taught common soldiers, that common soldiers taught officers, that officers taught field commanders, that field commanders taught their desk-bound superiors in Washington, and that resonated in the North was not wasted on Abraham Lincoln. In many ways, Lincoln was a slow learner, but he learned.

Lincoln was no friend of slavery. He believed, as he said many times, that "if slavery is not wrong, nothing is wrong." But, as president, Lincoln also believed he had a constitutional obligation not to interfere with slavery where it existed. Shortly before his inauguration, he offered to support a proposed constitutional amendment that would have prohibited any subsequent amendment authorizing Congress "to abolish or interfere . . . with the domestic institutions" of any state, including slavery."[25] As wartime leader, he feared the disaffection of the loyal slave states, which he understood to be critical to the success of the Union. He crafted much of his wartime policy respecting slavery to avoid alienating loyal slaveholders, especially in Kentucky, Missouri, and Maryland. . . .

Where others led on emancipation, Lincoln followed. Lincoln responded slowly to demands for emancipation as they rose through the military chain of command and as they echoed on the Northern home front. Even as pressure for emancipation grew in the spring of 1862, Lincoln continued to urge gradual, compensated emancipation. The compensation would be to slaveholders for property lost, not to slaves for labor stolen. In late September 1862, even while announcing that he would proclaim emancipation on January 1 if the rebellious states did not return to the Union, he again called for gradual, compensated emancipation in the border states and compensation for loyal slaveholders elsewhere. The preliminary emancipation proclamation also reiterated his support for colonizing freed slaves "upon this con-

[25] For the proposed amendment, see ibid., 59; Abraham Lincoln, *Collected Works of Abraham Lincoln*, ed. Roy P. Basler, 9 vols. (New Brunswick, N.J.: Rutgers Univ. Press, 1953–55), 4:421–41 [Berlin note].

tinent or elsewhere."[26] While some pressed for the enlistment of black soldiers, Lincoln doubted the capacity of black men for military service, fearing that former slaves would simply turn their guns over to their old masters.

As black laborers became essential to the Union war effort and as demands to enlist black men in the Federal army mounted, the pressure for emancipation became inexorable. By the summer of 1862, Lincoln understood the importance of the sable arm as well as any. On July 12, making yet another plea for gradual, compensated emancipation in the Union's own slave states, Lincoln bluntly warned border-state congressmen that slavery was doomed "by mere friction and abrasion—by the mere incidents of the war," and that it would be impossible to restore the Union with slavery in place.[27] Ignored once again, Lincoln acted on his own advice. In late July 1862, five days after signing the Second Confiscation and the Militia acts, he issued an executive order translating the new legislation into instructions for the Union army and navy. He authorized military commanders operating in the seceded states to "seize and use any property, real or personal, which may be necessary or convenient for . . . military purposes," and he instructed them to "employ as laborers . . . so many persons of African descent as can be advantageously used for military and naval purposes." Although he also reiterated the customary injunctions against wanton or malicious destruction of private property, there was no mistaking the import of Lincoln's order.[28]

Lincoln had decided to act. On July 22, he informed the cabinet of his intention to issue a proclamation of general emancipation. The slaves' determination had indeed made every policy short of emancipation untenable.[29] . . .

On January 1, 1863, Lincoln fulfilled his promise to free all slaves in the states still in rebellion. Had another Republican been in Lincoln's place, that person doubtless would have done the same. Without question, some would have acted more expeditiously and with greater bravado. Without question, some would have acted more cautiously and with lesser resolve. In the end, Lincoln did what needed to be done. Others might be left behind; Lincoln would not. It does no disservice

---

[26] *U.S. Statutes at Large*, 12 (Washington, D.C.: GPO, 1863): 1267–68 [Berlin note].

[27] Lincoln, *Collected Works*, 5:317–19, quotation on p. 318 [Berlin note].

[28] Lincoln's executive order, dated July 22, 1862, was promulgated to the armies in the field by a War Department order dated August 16. *OR*, ser. 3, 2:397 [Berlin note].

[29] As Lincoln later put it, "No human power can subdue this rebellion without using the Emancipation lever as I have done." Lincoln, *Collected Works*, 7:499–502, 506–8, quotation on p. 507 [Berlin note].

to Lincoln—or to anyone else—to say that his claim to greatness rests upon his willingness to act when the moment was right.

When Lincoln finally acted, he moved with confidence and determination. He stripped the final Emancipation Proclamation of any reference to compensation for former slaveholders or colonization for former slaves.[30] He added provisions that allowed for the service of black men in the Union army and navy. The Proclamation opened the door to the eventual enlistment of more than 179,000 black men, most of them former slaves. More than anything else, the enlistment of black men, slave as well as free, transformed the Federal army into an army of liberation. At war's end, the number of black men in Federal uniform was larger than the number of soldiers in Lee's Army of Northern Virginia. Military enlistment became the surest solvent of slavery, extending to places the Emancipation Proclamation did not reach, especially the loyal slave states. Once slave men entered the Union army, they were free and they made it clear that they expected their families to be free as well. In March 1865, Congress confirmed this understanding and provided for the freedom of the immediate families of all black soldiers. Lincoln's actions, however tardy, gave force to all that the slaves had risked. The Emancipation Proclamation transformed the war in ways only the president could. After January 1, 1863, the Union army marched for freedom, and Lincoln was its commander.[31]

Lincoln understood the importance of his role, both politically and morally—just as the slaves had understood theirs.[32] Having determined to free the slaves, Lincoln declared he would not take back the Emancipation Proclamation even when military failure and political reversals threatened that policy. He repudiated his misgivings about the military

[30] Lincoln, who had declared in his second annual message to Congress, "I cannot make it better known than it already is, that I strongly favor colonization," never made another public appeal for the scheme. Don E. Fehrenbacher, "Only His Stepchildren: Lincoln and the Negro," *Civil War History* 30 (1974): 308 [Berlin note].

[31] At times, McPherson appears to argue that the preeminence of Lincoln's role in the process of emancipation derived from the simple fact that he was the Republican candidate, wartime president, and commander in chief of the Union army, for freedom could not be achieved without Southern secession, civil war, and Union victory. If that is the pith of the case, it is easy enough to concede. Indeed, the first sentence of *The Black Military Experience* asserts: "Freedom came to most American slaves only through force of arms" [Berlin note].

[32] Although he makes no case for the slaves' role in emancipation, Don Fehrenbacher reaches a similar conclusion respecting Lincoln's role. "Emancipation itself, as [Lincoln] virtually acknowledged, came out of the logic of events, not his personal volition, but the time and manner of its coming were largely his choice." "Only His Stepchildren," 306 [Berlin note].

abilities of black soldiers and became one of their great supporters. Lincoln praised the role of black soldiers in preserving the Union and ending chattel bondage and vowed not to "betray" them. The growing presence of black men in the Union army deepened Lincoln's commitment to emancipation. "There have been men who proposed to me to return to slavery the black warriors of Port Hudson & Olustee to . . . conciliate the South," Lincoln reflected in August 1864. "I should be damned in time & in eternity for doing so."[33] Lincoln later suggested that black soldiers might have the vote, perhaps his greatest concession to racial equality.[34] To secure the freedom that his proclamation had promised, Lincoln pressed for the final liquidation of slavery in the Union's own slave states where diehards obstructed and delayed. To that end and to write freedom into the nation's highest charter, Lincoln promoted passage of the Thirteenth Amendment, although he did not live to see its ratification.

The Emancipation Proclamation's place in the drama of emancipation is thus secure—as is Lincoln's. To deny it is to ignore the intense struggle by which freedom arrived. It is to ignore the Union soldiers who sheltered slaves, the abolitionists who stumped for emancipation, and the thousands of men and women who, like Lincoln, changed their minds as slaves made the case for universal liberty. Reducing the Emancipation Proclamation to a nullity and Lincoln to a cipher denies human agency just as personifying emancipation in a larger-than-life Great Emancipator denies the agency of the slaves and many others, and trivializes the process by which the slaves were freed. And, as in many other cases, process is critical. . . .

Emphasizing that emancipation was not the work of one hand underscores the force of contingency, the crooked course by which universal freedom arrived. It captures the ebb and flow of events which, at times, placed Lincoln among the opponents of emancipation and then propelled him to the forefront of freedom's friends. It emphasizes the clash of wills that is the essence of politics, whether it involves enfranchised legislators or voteless slaves. Politics, perforce, necessitates an on-the-ground struggle among different interests, not the unfolding of a single idea

[33] Lincoln, *Collected Works*, 7:499–502, 506–8, quotation on p. 507 [Berlin note].

[34] "I barely suggest for your private consideration," Lincoln wrote to the Unionist governor of Louisiana in March 1864, "whether some of the colored people may not be let in [to the suffrage]—as, for instance, the very intelligent, and especially those who have fought gallantly in our ranks. They would probably help," he added, "in some trying times to come, to keep the jewel of liberty within the family of freedom." Lincoln, *Collected Works*, 7:243 [Berlin note].

or perspective, whether that of an individual or an age. Lincoln, no less than the meanest slave, acted upon changing possibilities as he understood them. The very same events—secession and war—that gave the slaves' actions new meaning also gave Lincoln's actions new meaning. To think that Lincoln could have anticipated these changes—or, more strangely still, somehow embodied them—imbues him with a power over the course of events that no human being has ever enjoyed. Lincoln was part of history, not above it. Whatever he believed about slavery in 1861, Lincoln did not see the war as an instrument of emancipation.[35] The slaves did. Lincoln's commitment to emancipation changed with time because it had to. The slaves' commitment to universal freedom never wavered because it could not.

Complexity—contrary to McPherson—is not ambivalence or ambiguity. To tell the whole story, to follow that crooked course, does not diminish the clarity of an argument or mystify it into a maze of "nuance, paradox, or irony." Telling the entire tale is not a form of obfuscation. If done right, it clarifies precisely because it consolidates the mass of competing claims under a single head. Elegance or simplicity of argument is useful only when it encompasses all of the evidence, not when it excludes or narrows it.

In the perennial tests in which constituted authority searches for the voice of the people and when the people are testing the measure of their leaders, it is well to recall the relationship of both to securing freedom's greatest victory. In this sense, slaves were right in celebrating January 1, 1863, as the Day of Jubilee. As Loretta Hanes noted 130 years later, "It meant so much to people because it was a ray of light, the hope of a new day coming. And it gave them courage."[36] Indeed, the Emancipation Proclamation reminds all—both those viewing its faded pages and those studying it—that real change derives both from the actions of the

---

[35] If there is a tendency in one brand of social history to emphasize the agency of the disfranchised, there is a similar tendency in one brand of political history to emphasize the omnipotence and clairvoyance of the great leader. The hero sees farthest, first. While combating the former fallacy, McPherson succumbs to the latter. From the beginning of the war, McPherson maintains, "Lincoln demurred from turning the war for Union into a war for slavery because the war for Union united Northern people while premature emancipation would divide them and lose the war." Lincoln, in other words, understood the Civil War as a struggle for emancipation from the beginning. He waited, however, for the right moment to spring the news on those not quite as farseeing. "With an acute sense of timing," McPherson continues, "Lincoln first proclaimed emancipation only as a *means* to win the war (to gain moderate and conservative support) and ultimately as an *end*—to give America a new birth of freedom,' as Lincoln said at Gettysburg" [Berlin note].

[36] *USA Today*, Dec. 30, 1992 [Berlin note].

people and from the imprimatur of constituted authority. It teaches that "social" history is no less political than "political" history, for it too rests upon the bending of wills, which is the essence of politics, and that no political process is determined by a single individual. If the Emancipation Proclamation speaks to the central role of constituted authority—in the person of Abraham Lincoln—in making history, it speaks no less loudly to the role of ordinary men and women, seizing the moment to make the world according to their own understanding of justice and human decency. The connection between the two should not be forgotten.

A Chronology of Emancipation (1776–1876)

1776 Adoption of Declaration of Independence.

1777– Northern states adopt measures abolishing slavery, though most
1805 make abolition gradual, and there are still slaves in the North
until the outbreak of the Civil War in 1861.

1787 Drafting of U.S. Constitution, which includes measures protecting
slavery in the United States.

1791 Slave uprising begins in the French colony of St. Domingue.

1793 United States passes first Fugitive Slave Act.

1800 Gabriel Prosser leads failed slave uprising in Virginia.

1804 Haiti, formerly St. Domingue, becomes an independent republic.

1808 United States passes act abolishing the slave trade.

1820 Missouri Compromise prohibits slavery north of latitude 36°30' in
the territories of the Louisiana Purchase, acquired in 1803.

1822 Denmark Vesey leads failed slave revolt in South Carolina.

1829 Mexico abolishes slavery.

1831 Nat Turner rebellion in Virginia.

1833 England passes act abolishing slavery throughout its empire.

1846 Outbreak of Mexican-American War.

Wilmot Proviso, proposed by Senator David Wilmot to outlaw
slavery in land acquired from Mexico, fails to pass Congress.

1848 France abolishes slavery in its colonies.

1850 Compromise of 1850 includes a stronger fugitive slave law and the
admission of California as a free state.

1854 Passage of Kansas-Nebraska Act, which allows voters in those
territories to establish slavery there—even north of the line set
by the Missouri Compromise.

1854– "Bleeding Kansas": violence between antislavery and proslavery
1858 settlers over whether slavery will be established in the territory.

1856 *May 21* Sack of Lawrence, Kansas, by proslavery forces.

May 22 Beating of Massachusetts Senator Charles Sumner by South Carolina Congressman Preston S. Brooks.

May 24 Abolitionists led by John Brown kill five settlers near Pottawatomie Creek, Kansas.

1857 *Dred Scott* decision by U.S. Supreme Court declares that African Americans cannot be citizens and that the Missouri Compromise is unconstitutional.

1859 John Brown's raid on Harpers Ferry, Virginia.

1860 *November 6* Abraham Lincoln elected president.

December 20 South Carolina secedes from the Union.

1861 *January 9–February 1* Secession of Mississippi, Florida, Alabama, Georgia, Louisiana, and Texas.

February 4–9 Confederate States of America established with a constitution and president, Jefferson Davis.

March 2 Congress adopts and sends to states resolution for a constitutional amendment prohibiting federal interference with slavery in the southern states.

March 4 Abraham Lincoln inaugurated.

April 12 Confederate troops fire on Fort Sumter, South Carolina.

April 14 Lincoln calls for seventy-five thousand troops to suppress the rebellion.

April 17–May 20 Secession of Virginia, Arkansas, North Carolina, and Tennessee.

May 24 General Benjamin F. Butler at Fortress Monroe, Virginia, refuses to return fugitive slaves to owners; other Union commanders soon adopt Butler's "contraband" policy.

July 25 Congress passes Crittenden Resolution pledging that the war is only to preserve the Union and will not interfere with slavery where it exists.

August 6 Congress passes First Confiscation Act, allowing for seizure of slaves used in aid of the rebellion.

August 30 General John C. Frémont declares martial law in Missouri and declares all slaves in the state free.

September 11 Lincoln orders Frémont's proclamation modified to leave slavery in Missouri untouched.

1862 *March 13*   Congress passes act prohibiting military officials from returning fugitive slaves to owners in rebellion.

April 16   Lincoln signs act abolishing slavery in Washington, D.C., which appropriates $100,000 for the colonization of freed slaves abroad.

May 9   Union general David Hunter issues order emancipating slaves in South Carolina, Georgia, and Florida.

May 19   Lincoln issues proclamation revoking Hunter's order.

July 12   Lincoln meets with Border State representatives from Congress urging them to support legislation in their states providing for emancipation and promising them federal funds to compensate slaveowners and colonize ex-slaves.

July 17   Lincoln signs Militia Act, which authorizes the military to hire African Americans and to declare their freedom as well as the freedom of any of their family members whose owners are in rebellion. The Border States are exempted from the legislation.

Lincoln signs Second Confiscation Act, which allows for seizure of property and slaves belonging to anyone supporting the rebellion; authorizes recruitment of ex-slaves into military service; and appropriates $500,000 for colonization of freed slaves abroad.

July 22   Lincoln presents first draft of Emancipation Proclamation to his cabinet and accepts recommendation to wait for a Union military victory before issuing it.

August 14   Lincoln promotes colonization abroad to a delegation of African American leaders at the White House.

September 17   Union armies under General George B. McClellan halt Confederate invasion of Maryland at the Battle of Antietam.

September 22   Lincoln issues preliminary Emancipation Proclamation, which pledges to emancipate the slaves in rebellious areas on January 1, 1863, pledges federal compensation to slaveowners in states abolishing slavery immediately or gradually, and promises to continue to support plans to colonize ex-slaves abroad.

December 1   Lincoln sends annual message to Congress, which calls for amendments to the Constitution providing for gradual emancipation with compensation to slaveowners and colonization of ex-slaves.

1863 *January 1*   Lincoln issues final Emancipation Proclamation, freeing the slaves in all areas in rebellion except northern and western Virginia, southern Louisiana, and Tennessee.

May 22   War Department creates Bureau of Colored Troops.

July 1–3 Union army wins victory at Gettysburg.

July 13–16 New York City draft riots lead to violence against African American soldiers and civilians.

July 18 African American soldiers lead failed Union assault on Fort Wagner, South Carolina.

November 19 Lincoln delivers Gettysburg Address.

December 8 Lincoln issues Proclamation of Amnesty and Reconstruction, offering liberal terms of amnesty to former Confederates and reinstatement to the Union for states in rebellion.

1864 *April 8* Senate adopts resolution for a constitutional amendment abolishing slavery.

June 15 Congress makes pay of black soldiers equal to that of white soldiers.

House of Representatives fails to pass resolution for antislavery amendment to the Constitution.

July 2 Congress passes Wade-Davis bill, which declares slavery abolished in states in rebellion and provides stricter terms of amnesty and reconstruction than Lincoln offered in his proclamation of December 8, 1863. Lincoln pocket vetoes the bill.

October 13 Maryland votes to abolish slavery.

November 8 Lincoln reelected.

1865 *January 11* Missouri votes to abolish slavery.

January 12 Secretary of War Edwin M. Stanton and General William T. Sherman meet with African Americans in Savannah, Georgia, to discuss the future of the freed people.

January 16 General Sherman issues Special Field Order 15, specifying that confiscated land along the coast of South Carolina, Georgia, and Florida be settled by African Americans in forty-acre sections.

January 31 House of Representatives adopts resolution for Thirteenth Amendment abolishing slavery and sends it to the states for ratification.

March 3 Congress passes act extending Militia Act of 1862 to Border States: Families there of African Americans in the military now freed.

Congress passes act creating the Freedmen's Bureau to oversee African Americans' transition to freedom in the South.

March 13 Confederate Congress passes act authorizing the recruitment of slaves as soldiers; slaveowners' permission is required for recruitment, and slaves serving in the military are to be emancipated.

April 9   Confederate general Robert E. Lee surrenders to Union general Ulysses S. Grant at Appomattox Court House, Virginia.

April 14   Lincoln assassinated; he dies the next day, and Andrew Johnson becomes president.

December 18   Ratification of Thirteenth Amendment, abolishing slavery.

1868   Ratification of Fourteenth Amendment, securing citizenship and equal protection of the laws to African Americans.

1870   Ratification of Fifteenth Amendment, securing voting rights for African American men.

1876   Dedication of Freedmen's (or Emancipation) Memorial in Washington, D.C.

Questions for Consideration

1. How did various groups of people at the beginning of the Civil War understand the role of slavery in causing the war?

2. How did the actions of African Americans shape the Union's emancipation policy during the war?

3. If Lincoln had issued the Emancipation Proclamation (Document 21) at the start of the war, rather than in 1863, how might the course of the war have been different?

4. Did Lincoln exceed his presidential power in issuing the Emancipation Proclamation?

5. How do the two images of Lincoln drafting the Emancipation Proclamation by Edward Dalton Marchant and Adalbert Johann Volck (Documents 18 and 19) differ? What might explain the differences?

6. What accounts for the differences in both the form and content of the two images from *Harper's Weekly* (Documents 25 and 26) depicting African American reactions to emancipation?

7. If the creation of the Confederacy had been followed not by war but by peaceful coexistence between the United States and the Confederate States of America, how long do you think slavery would have lasted in each nation?

8. What factors were most important in the decision of the U.S. government to allow African Americans to serve in the armed forces?

9. How did military service enhance African Americans' claims to equal citizenship?

10. Why might Confederate authorities have believed that African Americans would be willing to fight for the Confederacy?

11. If southern leaders had approved the enlistment of African Americans in the Confederate armed forces earlier—perhaps in early 1864, when General Patrick R. Cleburne made his recommendation (Document 35)—how might the course of the war have been different?

12. What did freedom mean to newly emancipated African Americans, and how did their notions differ from those of Lincoln and other Union officials?

13. Was Frederick Douglass accurate when, in 1876, he called Lincoln the "white man's President" (Document 48)?

14. How do the two depictions of the moment of emancipation by the sculptor Thomas Ball and the artist Henry W. Herrick (Documents 49 and 50) reflect different understandings of the causes and meaning of African American freedom?

15. How do the arguments of James M. McPherson and Ira Berlin (Documents 51 and 52) differ, and is there any way to reconcile their positions?

Selected Bibliography

GENERAL WORKS ON EMANCIPATION, THE CIVIL WAR, AND ABRAHAM LINCOLN

Much has been published on the politics and experience of emancipation during the Civil War and Reconstruction. The best place to begin is the multivolume *Freedom: A Documentary History of Emancipation, 1861–1867* (Cambridge: Cambridge University Press, 1982–). Ira Berlin and the other editors of the series have also published a number of single-volume collections derived from the series. Of these, the two most useful are *Free at Last: A Documentary History of Slavery, Freedom, and the Civil War* (New York: New Press, 1992), which includes mostly original documents; and *Slaves No More: Three Essays on Emancipation and the Civil War* (Cambridge: Cambridge University Press, 1992), which is a set of scholarly essays based on the larger series. For a detailed study of the origins and impact of the Emancipation Proclamation, see Allen C. Guelzo, *Lincoln's Emancipation Proclamation: The End of Slavery in America* (New York: Simon & Schuster, 2004). For a briefer overview of the Proclamation, see John Hope Franklin, *The Emancipation Proclamation* (Garden City, N.Y.: Doubleday, 1963). On the role of abolitionists in Civil War emancipation, see James M. McPherson, *The Struggle for Equality: Abolitionists and the Negro in the Civil War and Reconstruction*, 2nd ed. (Princeton, N.J.: Princeton University Press, 1995). McPherson also edited a valuable documentary history of the struggle for emancipation and equal rights in the era: *The Negro's Civil War: How American Negroes Felt and Acted during the War for the Union*, 2nd ed. (Urbana: University of Illinois Press, 1985). On the relationship between Lincoln and African Americans, see John Stauffer, *Giants: The Parallel Lives of Frederick Douglass and Abraham Lincoln* (New York: Twelve, 2008); George M. Fredrickson, *Big Enough to Be Inconsistent: Abraham Lincoln Confronts Slavery and Race* (Cambridge, Mass.: Harvard University Press, 2008); James Oakes, *The Radical and the Republican: Frederick Douglass, Abraham Lincoln, and the Triumph of Antislavery Politics* (New York: Norton, 2007); LaWanda Cox, *Lincoln and Black Freedom: A Study in Presidential Leadership*, 2nd ed. (Urbana: University of Illinois Press, 1985); and Benjamin Quarles, *Lincoln and the Negro* (New York: Oxford University Press, 1962).

A work that is highly critical of Lincoln and his views on emancipation and racial equality is Lerone Bennett Jr., *Forced into Glory: Abraham Lincoln's White Dream* (Chicago: Johnson, 1999). A valuable collection of essays that assesses the arguments of Bennett and others is Brian R. Dirck, ed., *Lincoln Emancipated: The President and the Politics of Race* (De Kalb: Northern Illinois University Press, 2007). For general information on Abraham Lincoln, the best one-volume biography is David Herbert Donald, *Lincoln* (New York: Simon & Schuster, 1995).

SLAVERY AND THE COMING OF THE CIVIL WAR

The role of slavery in the lead-up to the Civil War is the subject of scores of books. Of these, the most relevant to the subject of emancipation during the Civil War and Reconstruction are Don E. Fehrenbacher, *The Slaveholding Republic: An Account of the United States Government's Relations to Slavery*, completed and edited by Ward M. McAfee (New York: Oxford University Press, 2001); Leonard L. Richards, *The Slave Power: The Free North and Southern Domination, 1780–1860* (Baton Rouge: Louisiana State University Press, 2000); and Richard H. Sewell, *Ballots for Freedom: Antislavery Politics in the United States, 1837–1860* (New York: Oxford University Press, 1976). For the turn to antislavery by white northerners in the antebellum era, see Eric Foner, *Free Soil, Free Labor, Free Men: The Ideology of the Republican Party before the Civil War*, 2nd ed. (New York: Oxford University Press, 1995). On northern African Americans and radical abolitionists during the period, see John Stauffer, *The Black Hearts of Men: Radical Abolitionists and the Transformation of Race* (Cambridge, Mass.: Harvard University Press, 2002); and Patrick Rael, *Black Identity and Black Protest in the Antebellum North* (Chapel Hill: University of North Carolina Press, 2002). For the rise of southern sectionalism and proslavery thought, see William W. Freehling, *The Road to Disunion*, vol. 1, *Secessionists at Bay, 1776–1854* (New York: Oxford University Press, 1990); William W. Freehling, *The Road to Disunion*, vol. 2, *Secessionists Triumphant, 1854–1861* (New York: Oxford University Press, 2007); and Manisha Sinha, *The Counterrevolution of Slavery: Politics and Ideology in Antebellum South Carolina* (Chapel Hill: University of South Carolina Press, 2000).

THE IMPACT OF THE CIVIL WAR ON SLAVERY

Lincoln's election, southern secession, and the beginning of the Civil War all helped to begin to undermine slavery, a process detailed in Armstead L. Robinson, *Bitter Fruits of Bondage: The Demise of Slavery and the Collapse of the Confederacy, 1861–1865* (Charlottesville: University Press of Virginia, 2005). On the development and impact of confiscation policies that affected slavery, see Daniel W. Hamilton, *The Limits of Sovereignty: Property Confiscation in the Union and the Confederacy during the Civil War* (Chicago: University of Chicago Press, 2007); Silvana R. Siddali, *From Property to Person:*

Slavery and the Confiscation Acts, 1861–1862 (Baton Rouge: Louisiana State University Press, 2005); and Louis Gerteis, *From Contraband to Freedman: Federal Policy toward Southern Blacks, 1861–1865* (Westport, Conn.: Greenwood, 1973). On Union and Confederate soldiers' confrontation with slavery, see Chandra Manning, *What This Cruel War Was Over: Soldiers, Slavery, and the Civil War* (New York: Knopf, 2007). Legal issues concerning emancipation are detailed in Herman Belz, *Emancipation and Equal Rights: Politics and Constitutionalism in the Civil War Era* (New York: Norton, 1978); and Harold M. Hyman, *A More Perfect Union: The Impact of the Civil War and Reconstruction on the Constitution* (New York: Knopf, 1973). On the implications of the Emancipation Proclamation for U.S. foreign relations, see Howard Jones, *Abraham Lincoln and a New Birth of Freedom: The Union and Slavery in the Diplomacy of the Civil War* (Lincoln: University of Nebraska Press, 1999).

THE AFRICAN AMERICAN MILITARY EXPERIENCE

Dudley Taylor Cornish, *The Sable Arm: Negro Troops in the Union Army, 1861–1865*, 2nd ed. (Lawrence: University Press of Kansas, 1987), remains the best overview of African American service in the Union armed forces, but see also Benjamin Quarles, *The Negro in the Civil War*, 2nd ed. (New York: Russell and Russell, 1968). On African Americans in the Union navy, see Steven J. Ramold, *Slaves, Sailors, Citizens: African Americans in the Union Navy* (De Kalb: Northern Illinois University Press, 2002). The relationship between white officers and African American troops is the subject of Joseph T. Glatthaar, *Forged in Battle: The Civil War Alliance of Black Soldiers and White Officers* (New York: Free Press, 1990). A number of studies of southern regions or communities during the Civil War detail southern African Americans' transformation from slaves to soldiers. One of the most interesting of these is Ervin L. Jordan, *Black Confederates and Afro-Yankees in Civil War Virginia* (Charlottesville: University Press of Virginia, 1995). The Fifty-fourth Massachusetts Regiment has received more attention than any other African American fighting unit in the Civil War. Two edited collections are invaluable in the study of the Fifty-fourth: Donald Yacovone, *A Voice of Thunder: The Civil War Letters of George E. Stephens* (Urbana: University of Illinois Press, 1997), which reprints many of the letters of Stephens, a soldier and a correspondent of New York's *Anglo-American*; and Russell Duncan, ed., *Blue-Eyed Child of Fortune: The Civil War Letters of Colonel Robert Gould Shaw* (Athens: University of Georgia Press, 1992), which reprints correspondence of the regiment's commander.

CONFEDERATE EMANCIPATION

Two major works study the debate in the Confederacy over emancipating and arming African Americans: Bruce C. Levine, *Confederate Emancipation: Southern Plans to Free and Arm Slaves during the Civil War* (New York:

Oxford University Press, 2005); and Robert F. Durden, *The Gray and the Black: The Confederate Debate on Emancipation* (Baton Rouge: Louisiana University Press, 1972).

RECONSTRUCTION

Emancipation was not completed until Reconstruction; therefore, works on Reconstruction are crucial to understanding the evolution of emancipation from a wartime policy to a social reality. The best overview of Reconstruction is Eric Foner, *Reconstruction: America's Unfinished Revolution, 1863–1877* (New York: Harper & Row, 1988), but also useful are studies of specific southern communities. Of these, the most relevant examine areas where reconstruction began during the war, overseen by Union occupying authorities: John C. Rodrigue, *Reconstruction in the Cane Fields: From Slavery to Free Labor in Louisiana's Sugar Parishes, 1862–1880* (Baton Rouge: Louisiana State University Press, 2001); Julie Saville, *The Work of Reconstruction: From Slave to Wage Laborer in South Carolina, 1860–1870* (Cambridge: Cambridge University Press, 1994); and Willie Lee Rose, *Rehearsal for Reconstruction: The Port Royal Experiment* (New York: Oxford University Press, 1976). On Lincoln and the politics of emancipation under Reconstruction, see Michael Vorenberg, *Final Freedom: The Civil War, the Abolition of Slavery, and the Thirteenth Amendment* (Cambridge: Cambridge University Press, 2001); William C. Harris, *With Charity for All: Lincoln and the Restoration of the Union* (Lexington: University Press of Kentucky, 1997); and Herman Belz, *Reconstructing the Union: Theory and Policy during the Civil War* (Ithaca, N.Y.: Cornell University Press, 1969). On the role of Frederick Douglass during the Civil War and Reconstruction, including his relationship with Lincoln, see David W. Blight, *Frederick Douglass' Civil War: Keeping Faith in Jubilee* (Baton Rouge: Louisiana State University Press, 1989). On the contested place of emancipation in the memory of the Civil War, see David W. Blight, *Race and Reunion: The Civil War in American Memory* (Cambridge, Mass.: Harvard University Press, 2001). On the eclipse of the Emancipation Proclamation by the Gettysburg Address in American memory, see Gabor S. Boritt, *The Gettysburg Gospel: The Lincoln Speech That Nobody Knows* (New York: Simon & Schuster, 2006).

Acknowledgments (continued from p. iv)

Documents 1, 2, 3, 5, 8, 14, 15, 20, 21, 43, 45, 46: Roy P. Basler, ed., and Marion Dolores Pratt and Lloyd A. Dunlap, asst. eds., *The Collected Works of Abraham Lincoln*, 8 vols. (New Brunswick, N.J.: Rutgers University Press, 1953–1955), permission courtesy of the Abraham Lincoln Association, Springfield, Illinois.

Document 51: "Who Freed the Slaves?" Copyright 1996 by James M. McPherson, used by permission of the author.

Document 52: Ira Berlin, "Who Freed the Slaves? Emancipation and Its Meaning," in David W. Blight and Brooks D. Simpson, eds., *Union and Emancipation: Essays on Politics and Race in the Civil War Era* (Kent, Ohio: Kent State University Press, 1997), 105–21, with permission of The Kent State University Press.

Index

abolitionism/abolitionists
  African American, 46–47, 56–58, 72–73
  criticism of Lincoln's moderate policies, 52, 54–58
  defeat of, in South, 3
  Douglass's split with, 119–20
  in Europe, 3–4
  formal political actions of, 5
  impact of fugitive slave laws on, 7
  Lincoln's response to activism of, 5
  northern emancipation measures, 3
  northern strategies, 4–5
  Republican Party and, 8–9
  response to Proclamation, 53
  violent opposition to, 5, 109
  war against slavery and, 142
"Abraham Lincoln" (Marchant), 64–65
Adams, John Quincy, 5, 16
"Address to the People of the Confederate States" (Congress of the Confederate States of America), 97–98
African Americans
  abolitionism of, 46–47, 56–58, 72–73
  American Freedmen's Inquiry Commission and, 106–8
  "black laws" and, 5, 12, 73
  colonization plans for, 13–14, 15–16, 50, 60, 67–68, 79, 146–47, 155
  in contraband camps, 105–6
  forced apprenticeships for, 3
  land redistribution policy for, 117–19, 156
  legal equality for, 19, 20, 22–23, 24, 53, 111–12, 119–20
  in postwar South, 23, 117–19
  racism against, 12–13, 108–9, 156
  response to colonization plans, 15–16
  response to Lincoln's election, 10
  response to Proclamation, 72–73, 122
  voting rights for, 23, 115–16, 120, 149
  See also African Americans, in military; equal rights, for African Americans; slaves

African Americans, in military, 79–92
  Confederate debate over enlisting, 21–22, 41–42, 93–103
  Confederate execution of prisoners, 19, 84–86
  Confederate troops, 102
  dangers faced by, 80
  debate over suitability for combat, 18, 50–51, 56, 79
  Douglass on, 81–83
  Emancipation Proclamation and, 17–18, 80–81, 148
  government authorization for, 11–12, 17–18, 50–51, 147, 155
  hopes for legal equality for, 80, 82–84, 85–86
  as laborers, 11–12, 18, 50–51, 79, 142–45, 147
  liberation of family members by, 91–92
  Lincoln on fair treatment of, 19, 85, 104, 149
  numbers in Union forces, 18, 79–80, 143
  racist policies and practices, 19, 79, 82
  treatment of families of, 12, 20, 80, 86–87, 148
  unequal payment for, 19, 79, 82, 89–91, 156
  in Union all-white regiments, 79, 80
  Union enlistment and regiments, 18, 19, 54, 79, 88, 89–91, 143, 148, 156
African Methodist Episcopal (AME) Church, 117
American Colonization Society, 13
American Freedmen's Inquiry Commission, 106–8
American Party, 7–8
American Revolution, 138
Anderson, Robert, 46*n*
Andrew, John A., 82
Anglo-African, 83, 89
"Annual Message to Congress" (Lincoln), 53, 67–70

165